2114

⊂

# Darling

ALSO BY RICHARD RODRIGUEZ

*Hunger of Memory: The Education of Richard Rodriguez*

*Days of Obligation: An Argument with My Mexican Father*

*Brown: The Last Discovery of America*

# Darling

*a spiritual autobiography*

RICHARD RODRIGUEZ

*viking*

VIKING
Published by the Penguin Group
Penguin Group (USA) LLC
375 Hudson Street
New York, New York 10014

USA | Canada | UK | Ireland | Australia | New Zealand | India | South Africa | China
penguin.com
A Penguin Random House Company
First published by Viking Penguin, a member of Penguin Group (USA) LLC, 2013

Acknowledgments to publishers of previously published chapters appear on page xi.

Grateful acknowledgment is made for permission to reprint excerpts from the following copy-
righted works:

*Hell* by Kathryn Davis. Copyright © 2003 by Kathryn Davis. Used by permission of The Wylie
    Agency LLC.
"The Crack-Up" from *The Crack-Up* by F. Scott Fitzgerald. Copyright © 1945 by New Directions
    Publishing Corp. Reprinted by permission of New Directions Publishing Corp.
"The Enchanted" from *Four Plays* by Jean Giraudoux. Copyright © 1948, 1950 by Maurice Valency.
    Reprinted by permission of Hill and Wang, a division of Farrar, Straus and Giroux, LLC.
*The Daring Young Man on the Flying Trapeze* by William Saroyan. By permission of The Stanford
    University Libraries.
*The Stone Diaries* by Carol Shields. Copyright © Carol Shields, 1993. Published by Viking, a mem-
    ber of Penguin Group (USA) LLC.

Library of Congress Cataloging-in-Publication Data

Rodriguez, Richard.
    Darling : a spiritual autobiography / Richard Rodriguez.
      pages cm
    ISBN 978-0-670-02530-5
    1. Rodriguez, Richard, 1944–  2. Catholic Church—United States—Biography.
3. Christian pilgrims and pilgrimages—Israel.  4. United States—Religion.  I. Title.
    BX4705.R6375A3 2013
    282.092—dc23
    [B]

                                2013017046

Printed in the United States of America
10  9  8  7  6  5  4  3  2

Set in Palatino
Designed by Carla Bolte

*For the Sisters of Mercy of the Americas*

# A Note to the Reader

All the chapters within were written in the years after September 11, 2001—years of religious extremism throughout the world, years of rising public atheism, years of digital distraction. I write as a Christian, a Roman Catholic. My faith in the desert God makes me kin to the Jew and the Muslim.

Throughout, and especially in the chapter "Darling," I have altered many names and fictionalized some events and locations.

Hugo House, a writers' workshop in Seattle, solicited the chapter called "Tour de France"; it was reprinted in the *Kenyon Review*. The *Wilson Quarterly* published the chapter on Cesar Chavez, "Saint Cesar of Delano." *California*, the alumni magazine of the University of California, Berkeley, first published "Disappointment." "Final Edition" appeared in *Harper's Magazine*. *Harper's* also published an earlier version of the chapter that appears here as "Jerusalem and the Desert." A two-page sketch of the final chapter, "The Three Ecologies of the Holy Desert," was first printed in *Image*.

# Contents

# Darling

# one

## *Ojalá*

One summer evening in London, many years ago, I was walking through green twilight in Hyde Park when I attracted the gaze of a large woman who was wearing several coats; she was tending to two children, a girl and a boy—her grandchildren, I surmised. As I passed, the woman posted a radiant, recognizing smile. "Arabie?" she asked.

I smiled, too. I shook my head, as though sadly. *No.*

Now I am not so sure.

In the predawn dark, a young man is bobbing up and down behind the pillar of an airport lounge a few yards from my departure gate. I watch from behind my newspaper. The man turns in a circle before the floor-to-ceiling window, beyond which an airliner lumbers upward like a blue whale to regain the suspended sea. The young man cups his hands behind his ears, then falls out of sight.

One other passenger sees what I see. "Someone should call the police," the woman says out loud, not to me, not to anyone—a thought balloon.

To say what? A Muslim is praying at Gate 58.

In the final months of my parents' lives—months of wheelchairs heaved into the trunks of cars, months of desperate clutchings at handrails and car doors—I often drove them to the five-thirty Mass on Saturday evenings.

One Saturday in mid-September 2001—a day without fog, a warm evening sky—I steered my mother's wheelchair out of the church, careful of the radius of the thing, careful of her toes. All of us at Mass felt a need for congregation that evening. In the interval between last Saturday and this, we had learned something terrible about the nature of religion.

Several women of the parish leaned over my mother's wheelchair, as they often did. A few months hence, when my mother could no longer leave the house, these same women would ring the doorbell of my parents' house to bring Holy Communion to my mother.

*Terrible times,* the women murmured among themselves, all of them in tropically colored blouses. *Terrible, terrible times!*

Something had happened in the sky. In a way it was more extraordinary than a mystic's vision—the vision, for example, of Caryll Houselander, the English artist, writer, bohemian. London, 1918: Houselander, a young woman of sixteen, was on her way to buy potatoes for her family's dinner. She knew she must not tarry on the way home. Suddenly, above her, as she recounts, "wiping out not only the grey street and sky but the whole world," was an icon of Christ the King crucified. Houselander goes on to explain, as all mystics must but never can explain, that she saw with her mind's eye.

We of the congregation had not seen with our minds' eyes, but through our television screens. We saw people—they were so far away but we knew they were people, they were not cinders or the leaves of calendars; we saw people who had no alternative but to consign their bodies—their bodies, I say, but I mean their lives—

to the air, people who are loved, I believe, by God, even as I believe their murderers are loved by God. Falling.

A friend of mine, a Jew, called at about that time to ask if there was ever a time when I did not believe in God. My answer was no. Her answer was no also.

It was in the weeks following the terrorist attacks of September 11 that I came to the realization that the God I worship is a desert God. It was to the same desert God the terrorists prayed.

The cockpit terrorists believed, furthermore, that God is honored by violent death, by the violent deaths of the hapless people who worked in those towering buildings, or who were visiting there, or delivering something on that particular day, at that particular hour.

I do not believe what the destroyers believed—that God is honored by a human oath to take lives. I do not believe God can be dishonored. The action of the terrorists was a human action, conceived in error—a benighted act. And yet I worship the same God as they, so I stand in some relation to those men.

I long have assumed, as a Christian, a Roman Catholic (by the favor of colonial Mexico), that I am a younger brother to the Jew, because the Jew and I worship the same God, and the Hebrew Bible is mine also, though less mine—*cf.* Jesus Christ: *Salvation is from the Jews.* For most of my life, though, I have scarcely regarded the Muslim—despite centuries of Muslim rule of Spain, a country to which (by the favor of colonial Mexico) I am related; and despite the fact that Brother Dennis, classroom 119, Christian Brothers High School, Sacramento, 1962, famously opined that Islam is, indeed, "a true religion"; and despite the fact that the Muslim claims Abraham as father, as does the Jew, as do I.

As increasing numbers of Muslims declare war in their hearts against "Crusaders and Zionists," I endeavor to put away my ignorance about Muslims. War is one of the most intimate human behaviors. Soldiers know it. Boxers know it. Schoolchildren know it. Adversaries grow as preoccupied with one another as do young lovers. The general must try to imagine the battlefield the other way around, like a hairdresser working in a mirror. Thus am I drawn to the customs and thoughts of the one who threatens me. I strain to hear what he is saying about me among his confreres.

The first Arabic word I learned in the aftermath of September 11 was *jihad*.

Despite the suspicion with which Americans regarded Jewish and Catholic immigrants in the nineteenth century, despite the persecution of Mormons, Americans are unaccustomed to thinking of a religious war as having anything at all to do with us. Religious wars happen elsewhere. Religious wars happened long ago. Saracens and so forth. Albigensians. And yet the legend of our nation's founding concerns Puritans seeking refuge from religious persecution in England and finding that refuge on the shore of the North American continent.

At the dawn of a worldwide religious war that Americans prefer to name a war against terror, I feel myself drawn to Islam, drawn to read the Koran, even to kiss the Koran—melodramatically, but sincerely—as I did one evening recently in front of a university audience. I meant to honor Islam. I meant to convey that, as a Christian, I consider myself a loving brother to the Muslim, as I am to the Jew, by the favor of Father Abraham.

In the months after September 11, at various international airports, I found myself facing security officers in glass booths who fastidiously turned the pages of my passport, as though they were reading. But they were not reading. Their eyes did not leave my face.

*Don't look evasive don't look steely don't look sly.*

The inked tongue of the stamp machine was held suspended over my passport all the while, but then it was put aside. I was directed to accompany another officer to a no-man's-room for a second scrutiny.

I am looking at a photograph of members of the bin Laden family of Saudi Arabia. They are on holiday in Sweden. It is 1971—nearly ten years after Brother Dennis's ratification of Islam—a bland, sunny day. The young men and women in the photograph are smiling; they pose in front of a pink Cadillac limousine; they are dressed in the mode of Carnaby Street. These young bin Ladens are, for the moment, at ease in a jolly old world.

But one among the bin Laden heirs is missing from the photograph; one has a spirit that wants to concentrate, to contract, rather than to absorb.

Thirty years after the Sweden photograph, the face of Osama bin Laden appears on every television news show, every magazine cover, every newspaper, in the world. Bin Laden smiles benignly. His brown eyes observe the mechanics of my nightmare from the obverse, as a choragus would. He sees all the props. He sees bindles of hundred-dollar bills; he sees passports, airline tickets, box cutters. He watches as Internet commands burn through fiber-optic cables; he sees a peerless blue sky. He foresees his own smile, holy jubilation, dancing brothers, brothers dancing. He anticipates the pleasure of Allah.

The young terrorists whom Osama bin Laden dispatched into

the twenty-first century had some acquaintance with the West. They knew several languages, foremost among them the language of technology. At some point in their lives, they had discovered a wish or an imperative to separate themselves from their own human desires. They were trained to move between the snares of the devil and to maintain their resolve to kill the people they passed among. (*Look them in the eye. Do not look sly. Smile.*)

Hi.

September 10, 2001. Imagine the heartsickness of these young men, imagine the leaky bowels, the frequent swallowings, the swollen tongues, the reflexive yawns. Imagine the bathroom of a Days Inn as your chapel of vigil, where you sanctify yourself through the "Last Night." Imagine the sickening ablutions you are instructed by your captain to make: the shaving of hair from your body, the cloying scent of cologne, the prayers whispered into the palms of your hands and then applied to your secret body, like the blessings your mother long ago placed on you. Imagine the wish to flee.

When you emerge from your hotel room at dawn, you will be a crusader, impersonating a Crusader. Become what you hunt.

I send for a language course in Arabic because I want to hear what they are saying. I want to hear their quarrel with me. I want to taste their curses on my tongue; I want to imitate the posture of their prayers. I yearn to hear the strange heckling voice of God. Anyway, the software is incompatible with my computer. I call the number for technical support. I am connected to an aural hive that sounds like a train station in Delhi. I talk to a succession of optimistic young men in a room full of optimistic young men, all named Sayyid, all schooled in patience.

I realize I am unable to learn Arabic because I am unable to learn computer-ese. The power the young have over the old is the spirit of an age. In our age, technology is optimism. Technology is a new kind of democracy, supplanting borders. Nothing to memorize, only connect. I doubt if Sayyid would be able to afford the complicated computer system my computer quack has set up for me. But Sayyid understands it, which I never will.

Because I am unable to follow the simplest instructions over the phone, Sayyid asks permission to "enter" my computer. "I will set up a chat line so you can ask me questions while I work."

I do not avail myself of the chat line. Files appear. Bars race across the screen like bullet trains. Files topple into the trash. *Ding.* A message from Sayyid:

THERE YOU GO.

WHAT DO I DO?

CLICK THE ICON AND GO TO LESSON ONE.

*Lesson One: Bintoon. A girl. Waladoon. A boy.*

The power the old exert over the young is the power to send the young to war—flesh in its perfection dropped into a hellish maze of stimulus and response in order to defend an old man's phrase. A phrase! What? The American way of life? Yes. It galls me to say it, but yes. This paragraph costs me nothing. And yet I know it cost the life of a boy or a girl with a ready body and a mind not ripe. No one will come to question me this evening.

Often young American soldiers from Kansas or Arizona, upon being dispatched to the desert, speak of entering into the Bible. The terrain they mean. The tribal dress. Away in a manger.

We six-o'clock newsers have become accustomed to hearing the distant voices calling to us from the craters of bombed cities— *Allah akbar,* the voices cry. We understand what they are saying, young men writhing on gurneys. They are saying: *Mama! Help me! Save me! Kill them! God have mercy!*

In the no-man's-room at the Toronto airport, an old man— probably younger than I am—murmured *Salam Ahlaykom* when I sat beside him on a yellow plastic chair facing a blinded window.

I suppose I do look Arabic. No, you know what? I don't look Arabic—not if you know what you're looking at. In the eyes of border guards, my features are kind of floaty. Indeterminacy is possible grievance in the eyes of border guards.

The Muslim terrorist with his backpack slung on one shoulder arrives at the gate at Logan International Airport. He is an American college student en route to California, where, perhaps, it will be sunny and warm later today.

*Hi.*


During America's notorious sixties, I remember hearing some young Mexican Americans righteously foretell the Mexican *reconquista* of the southwestern United States. It was only a matter of time, these young people said, and sincerely believed, before history would bite its own tail; before ascending birthrates in Phoenix or Dallas would herald a just conclusion to the Mexican-American War.

Such a prediction was soon trampled by increasing numbers of immigrants arriving in the American Southwest, fleeing the civic failure of Mexico, certainly not seeking to perpetuate Mexico's influence in time or territory.

The dream of *reconquista* assumes that history revolves, that historical patterns are circles, even that a certain narrative point can be applied to history, like poetic justice, karma, Pyrrhic victory, irony. I think the circular clock face encourages us to think roundly—a finite numerology (Roman numerals, Arabic numerals) of 12 or 24; the tilt of Earth, the revolving seasons, the orderly succession of the sky. In the Digital Age, the age we have entered, time is no longer counted as recurrence but is cast forward to the unmaking of glaciers, the starvation of continents, the extinction of species.

I was sitting—beneath a clock, as a matter of fact; an old-fashioned pendulum clock with Roman numerals—in a student café near the Universidad Complutense de Madrid. I listened as a North African student predicted to me the Muslim reconquest of Europe. And his prediction, too, seemed a kind of circularity. He cited ascending birthrates of Muslim immigrants and declining birthrates of native Europeans. Europe is disappearing, he said. He foresaw a Muslim Paris, a Muslim Vienna, a Muslim Madrid— Muslims sleeping in the cradles, Muslims warming themselves at the firesides, Muslims filling the boulevards of a faithless, childless Europe. The earnest young man imagined the interrupted era of Muslim influence in Europe, a medieval golden age of tolerance and algebra and clock making, would be restored by the will of Allah. The young man's Spanish was better than mine.

My skepticism concerning all notions of *reconquista* is skepticism toward the view that history is restorative. I get older but I do not grow wiser. It is only by shedding skin, by turning pages, by ordering stronger spectacles, by having my hair cut, that I seem to be restoring myself to a circular pattern, that I seem to progress toward youth and capability, though my progress is actually a decline.

I seem to be forgetting something as my eyes weaken and my patience sharpens into a desperate, childish hunger: I am forgetting that one must become as a little child. (To reach the kingdom of Heaven, in Jesus's formulation. Or to apprehend an intuition of that kingdom—surely that is to believe in circularity?)

I seem to be missing rooms and days, days so tall I could not see an end to them. I miss persons who no longer exist.

Oh, c'mon, Frank, at least leave it up till New Year's Day.

What miracle of neuron and synapse allows one to laugh out loud in remembrance of a moment so long past? I see Frank (with my mind's eye); I hear Frank's sugar-cured voice. Frank is my landlord. How he amuses me! I watch Frank pluck a red bow and a pert artificial bird from an evergreen wreath and then dump the wreath into a trash bag.

*I'll tell you something, Richard: There's nothing so over as Christmas.* (December 26, perhaps 1985.)

Twenty-five years later, this same Frank woke to see his adored older brother, Cassius, standing in the doorway of the hospital room where Frank was taken after his last bedroom fall. Cassius was in his air force uniform, looking exactly as he had that summer morning in Birmingham, sixty years earlier, when Cassius paused in Frank's bedroom doorway before he turned and left for the war. *Cassius? Are you here or am I there?* But Cassius could not see Frank, or, if he could, he could not speak.

On a television documentary I watched last night, a Chilean astronomer said that the calcium in our bones is made of stardust. He was not speaking metaphorically.

Those who are old claim the advantage of far sight. The older you get, the more you remember; the more you forget, the more you regret. The more you sift. There remains the problem of reliability. My friend Florence: Florence is ninety-two. She cannot remember what she had for lunch or even . . . she looks at her watch . . . she supposes she must have had lunch by this time. Yet her mind can recall a day in 1925, a spring day: the back door is standing open because the kitchen is too warm. She can see a quarter moon with a pointed chin on the page of the calendar as she opens the back door for her mother, who is too warm; her mother preparing the Sabbath meal. The meal is going to be spoiled because her father and her eldest brother will quarrel; their father will leave the table. Florence shrugs. She forgets what point she was illustrating with the calendar, the too-warm kitchen, the anger of men.

I catch a glimpse of my mother through the doorway of our kitchen. I am just about to leave for school; it must be cold—I am zipping up my jacket, my binder between my knees. "See you later, Mama."

*Ojalá,* my mother calls.

My mother appended *ojalá* to every private leave-taking; my father never did. I heard the Spanish expression pristinely—I had heard it all my life. *Ojalá* meant *ojalá*. If I'd had the best friend I dreamed about, someone who would follow me about, who would want to know what everything meant, I would have told him *ojalá* means something like *I pray it may be so*—an exclamation and a petition.

Growing up, I thought the American expression *God willing and the creek don't rise* to be a variant of my mother's *ojalá*, which it is. I learned only this year, however, that the expression refers to Creek Indians, rather than to a swollen waterway.

In fact, the name of Allah was enshrined in the second and third syllables of my mother's *ojalá*. I doubt my mother knew that, though maybe she did. I didn't. The expression is a Spanish borrowing from the Arabic commonplace prayer *Insha'Allah*—God willing.

The nun stands apart as the women coalesce about my mother's wheelchair after Mass; she waits for the miasma of parrot-colored blouses to clear before she approaches. The nun's job is to minister to the elderly of the parish. She knows every old person by name;

she knows their children's names. She knows my name. I remember to ask after the health of her brother, who is ill in a town in southern Italy.

*Not so good. I hope to visit him this winter.*

Four months later, at the hospital where my father lay sunk in a coma, the Italian nun, whose brother had somewhat improved, stood at the foot of the bed, next to where my mother was seated. "We remain optimistic," my mother implored the nun. My desperate mother.

*Leo is dying, Victoria,* the nun said.

My mother tried to remove her hand from the nun's hand. The nun would not release her.

*We need to pray for Leo,* the nun said.

Oh, my poor mother. Proud as a mare, fiery as a mare, and now as frightened as a mare, my mother relinquished her spirit to the nun's calm instruction; she bowed her head and prayed like a schoolgirl for the old man who had been her husband for seventy years.

A year later, my mother died.

As many as four thousand Spanish words derive from Arabic. In 1492, when Columbus sailed the blue, when the Moor and the Jew were, by order of the Crown, expelled from Spain, Barbary already peppered the tongues of Spaniards.

Spaniards took Arabic words, or variants of remembered Arabic words, to the New World and salted the raw backs of Indians with them or whispered them in lust. So that, five centuries later, my Mexican mother, as a sort of reflex, would call upon Allah to keep the expected structure of her world intact. *Ojalá, Mama.* If the department store sale is still on. If the fog lifts. If it doesn't rain. If the results are negative. If we are all here next Christmas.

A characterization I have heard in recent years, at academic conferences on the Middle East, is that Christianity is a religion of guilt; Islam is a religion of grievance. Difference among the desert religions, rather than commonality, is the point drawn.

The argument proceeds: The theoretical Christian is weighed down by the knowledge of Original Sin. (If I were a young man, I would swear to you that I have never met a Christian who is weighed down by the knowledge of Original Sin. At my present age, I will tell you I have never met any human being who is not weighed down by the knowledge that men and women must fail.) The theoretical Christian inclines toward self-recrimination, which is reckoned a good thing, because self-recrimination is a corrective to anger. The theoretical Muslim knows no such fetters in his theology. The Prophet Muhammad rejected the notion of Original Sin. In the version of Islam that Western academics dispense at conferences, *jihad* is holy in the Koran and grievance can be expiated only by retribution.

Political theorists at secular academic conferences largely refrain (in my experience) from characterizing Judaism, though both Islam and Christianity are fractures of Judaism, glosses on Judaism, branches of Judaism—Judaism the root.

I must tell you: As a Christian, I am not flattered to hear academics describe the readiness of Christians to accept their guilt as a superior asset for living among people of disparate beliefs. It seems to me that Christians have inclined often enough, in our history, to harbor grievance. But it makes me uneasy to hear any academic assessment that implies that Christians are better equipped to live in a secular society than Muslims. As an American, I have never found an easy rhyme between my religion and my patriotism. Indeed, my religious life—born Mexican Catholic and raised Irish Catholic—has often been at odds with my

American faith in new beginnings. Even that wonderful phrase, "new beginnings," seems to me less a redundancy than a kind of tonic baptism, like Coca-Cola.

New beginnings: Grandma Moses said that if she ever got so down on her luck she couldn't make ends meet, why, then, she'd rent a church hall on credit and make pancakes. Maybe charge fifty cents. I don't know what it is about pancakes, she said, but if you make them, people will always come.

America is a faith, perhaps pancakes its sacrament. Opportunity comes to those who put away the disadvantages of family or circumstance and entrust themselves to the future. The point of the American story is simple enough for a child, particularly an immigrant child, to grasp: The past holds no sway in America.

Complicating my American faith, however, was the circumstance that Catholics—like high-church Protestants and like many Jews—describe themselves religiously by reference to the past and to the Old World. Regardless of any national variant of Catholicism (like Irish or Mexican), we are universal in faith— *Roman* Catholics, my Church taught me to say.

Don't you think it curious that so many Americans characterize their religious lives with reference to foreign allegiances? We are Dutch Reform; we are the Russian or the Greek Orthodox, or the Armenian or Syrian; we are the Russian, or the Galician, or the German, Jews; we are German Lutherans; we are Anglo Catholics; we belong to the Church of England! Even those Puritans of old who so famously sailed away from the intolerable Church of England ended up on the windy shore of Massachusetts, clutching their cloaks about them, gazing forlornly from history books that name them "English Puritans."

Richard Rodriguez wanted no accent in his voice, no ethnic shadow to his progress. Nevertheless, his Church educated Richard to imagine himself connected to a past much older than American optimism.

The odd thing is how well I remember my Roman youth, how well I remember the first of my Popes in the 1940s and '50s. That would be the forbidding Pope, Pius XII, with the beautifully molded head, the hook nose, the spectacles, the pewter complexion—all the more forbidding when he was laid out dead in the pages of *Life* magazine. He was a historical enigma, my first Pope. After more than fifty years, I am filled with the same dread looking at those photographs of him, and with a kind of heart-sickness, for I think I really did love that dark man.

Pius XII, John XXIII, Paul VI—the roster unrolls with the century. My American childhood passed from Harry Truman to Dwight D. Eisenhower to John F. Kennedy. Castel Gandolfo was as much a part of my imagination as Camp David.

Americans experience time in two distinct ways—as religious people and as people of no religion. Just so, we experience ourselves as a historical people and as people who are not implicated by history.

Being an American and being religious did not, early on, seem a conflict to me; these were two distinct ways of being, like school and summer. I read fewer lives of the saints than I read books about American heroes—inventors, presidents, explorers. I read the life of Saint Thérèse of Lisieux as well as the life of Louis Pasteur, her contemporary, her countryman. I assumed pasteurized milk was a boon to humankind. I assumed Saint Thérèse was praying for us, as she promised she would: *I will spend my heaven in doing good upon earth.*

With Mark Twain, I wondered at the incomprehensible ways of foreigners—myself an altar boy, a familiar of Latin prayers and incense and candles and images. I was still a number of years away from the more complicated versions of American innocence to be found in the fiction of Henry James, whose American heroine in Europe "blushed neither when she looked . . . nor when she felt that people were looking at her."

On my first day at college, a sophisticated young man, a Belgian, wandered into my dormitory room like a prince in a play, noticed the crucifix my mother had pinned to the lining of the suitcase I was unpacking, said: *I suppose you are a Roman.*

I was going to say my parents came from Mexico, but then I saw what he meant. Yes, I said, a Roman. And I realized it was true—that I had had an ulterior life for as long as I could remember.

I grew up during the changeover to Technicolor. Behind *Auntie Mame* and *Three Coins in the Fountain,* behind the draperies of scarlet and gold of the Second Vatican Council, lay the deserts of the Nuclear Age—the Holocaust, Hiroshima, the Soviet Gulag.

The recesses of my late-adolescent mind were black-and-white deserts—foreign films—for I grew up in the aftermath of the war, the Age of Pasolini, Bergman, and Fellini. The human face—Humanity—was a projection on a screen. Utterances from the face were sometimes inane, wreathed with smoke, discontinuous, lapsed (in foreign films continuity was not always an important consideration). The voice confounded the movement of the lips; the translator confounded the voice. After two wars, humanity was desperate to account for its survival.

I reached my majority in the Age of Freud, Joyce, Beckett, Auden, Eliot, Nabokov. The "New Criticism" was taught in colleges—the technique of approaching a work of literature as though literature exists in its own sphere, removed from history, biography, jealousy, the smell of the river. I prized artificiality over life—I had a great hunger to experience the portrayal of life, in books, in theater.

I grew up in the Age of Existentialism, whereby Man, capital *M*, is alone and free but without recourse to a crucifix that fills the sky. And yet all this café seriousness—you will have noticed—came from the Catholic world, from Europe. I was raised without much sense of trespass. Saint Thérèse easily coexisted with Samuel Beckett. Both spoke French. Both were harrowed by a world empty of God. One reinvented drama to accommodate an absence of meaning. One waited patiently as, in her own simile, a sparrow in a hedge waits for the fog to clear, for the sun to be revealed.

Pius XII, John XXIII, Paul VI, John Paul I . . . it became the habit of John Paul II to address the history of the Roman Catholic Church with contrition. The old man issued over ninety formal apologies—virtually a chronicle of Western civilization. He apologized for the Church's persecution of Galileo. He apologized for the Spanish Inquisition, for the persecution of Jews, for the mistreatment of Martin Luther, for the denigration of women; he apologized for the colonial mistreatment of Native peoples in the Americas; he apologized for violence against Orthodox Christians. John Paul II apologized to the Muslim world for the sacking of Constantinople by the Crusaders in 1204.

The Pope's penitential impulse coincided with a time in the history of the Church when fewer Roman Catholics, particularly in Europe and North America, were availing themselves of the sacrament of Penance. Penance is a sacrament out of line with the postmodern sensibility, for it seeks to alleviate sin—a word we no longer employ. In secular America, the holistic mode of self-forgiveness, self-dispensed, prevails. The pop-psych revivalism of afternoon television involves "owning" one's destructive behaviors; one embarks on a "healing path"; there follows a pledge, many tears, a commercial break. We are a Bathetic Age.

The U.S. government has apologized lately for a number of historical offenses—from slavery to the incarceration of American citizens of Japanese ancestry during World War II. But the truth is that we Americans are too individualistic to huddle together under a collective apology or a collective guilt. We don't understand what it means to apologize for the sins of a past generation. The American disclaimer: *I wasn't even born yet!*

As a Roman Catholic, I am prepared to say I am sorry for the Crusades. As an American, I hear some *Jihadist* curse American Crusaders—in English—as he passes in front of a BBC camera, and I am astonished because he implicates me.

As a Roman Catholic, I confess a past I had no part in, a past to which I adhere, a past that is shameful. But as soon as the old man sitting in the yellow plastic chair in the no-man's-room at the airport in Toronto starts going on about Crusader dogs, I think to myself: *Get over it, old man; you weren't even born yet!*

The two temples of my youth—of Rome, of America—were not unrelated. The first was my parish church—Sacred Heart Catholic Church, at 39th and J streets, in Sacramento. Sacred Heart Church remains one of the few figments of my dream life that survives and that I am able to revisit without disappointment. Within and without, the architecture is Romanesque—a Roman arch set with mosaic rises above the altar. The Harry Clarke Studio of Dublin City, Ireland, glazed the colored windows in the late 1920s.

My last year of grammar school coincided with the opening (again in the pages of *Life* magazine) of the Second Vatican Council and the desire of the "universal" Church to become, in the Pentecost metaphor of that era, "a Pilgrim Church on earth." The Church would henceforth speak in all the languages of the earth. My life became less Roman, thereby. The grandeur of the Latin

Mass was lost to me; my rhetorical exception from the naive American novel dissolved. At an early age, therefore, I experienced nostalgia. Nostalgia remains specific in my imagination: the Latin mass, the windows painted by the Harry Clarke Studio in Dublin, the German music favored by Anton Dorndorf, the parish's choir director. My nostalgia was for Europe.

It never occurred to me with any intellectual or emotional force until 2001—odd, because I had seen every Bible movie released between 1951 and 1964—that Christianity, like Judaism, like Islam, is a desert religion, an oriental religion, a Semitic religion, born of sinus-clearing glottal consonants, spit, dust, blinding light.

The Christian calendar has two "deserts"—Advent and Lent— two penitential preludes to the great feasts of Christmas and Easter. Though Christianity has sojourned so long in Europe that the penitential seasons are now imagined as seasons of gaunt— winters of the soul, rather than deserts. These expanses of cold time are symbolized by an ecclesiastical weather of purple cloth.

Which brings me to the second temple of my youth. The Alhambra Theatre in Sacramento was constructed in 1927 to resemble a tall white Muslim fortress. The Alhambra belonged to the generation of exotically themed movie houses that rivaled the fantasies people gathered to enjoy in them. In midsize towns and county seats across America, alongside the five-and-dimes and the Greco-Roman banks and the two-story department stores, there were neon-lit palaces, many with romantic themes derived from Spanish Arabia—the Alcazar, El Capitan, the Valencia, the Granada. Such palaces featured velvet proscenium curtains, wrought-iron balustrades, frescoes, starlit skies.

Roman days. We entered the Alhambra through a shaded garden. We walked among palms, alongside a reflecting pool, to reach the box office. On the screen, we saw sandal-shod feet, greaves laced to the bulging calves of Roman soldiers, raised standards of the legions of Caesar. A soundtrack of French horns and kettledrums bellowed like a herd of bullocks as marching troops kicked up the dust of some god-forsaken outback of empire. The camera found the eyes of Consul Stephen Boyd. We were relieved to be provided, at last, with a point of view. Stephen Boyd surveyed the desolation, raised his eyes to the balcony where I sat portioning a small box of Milk Duds to last through a crucifixion. A legend appeared in the center of the screen:

ANNO DOMINI

XXVI

I became a Christian at the Alhambra Theatre. I suppose I became a Crusader as well. On the screen of the Alhambra Theatre we watched Otto Preminger's *Exodus,* starring Paul Newman; we watched the blue eyes of Paul Newman survey the Mediterranean, espy the approach of the Promised Land, rising and falling, from the prow of the ship. It did not occur to me to imagine another point of view. I saw Palestine from the sea. I became a Zionist at the Alhambra Theatre.

The distance of Arabs from the American imagination made the ornate folly of the Alhambra Theatre possible. Before I was born, Rudolf Valentino caused a sensation playing the Sheik. Valentino was America's first exotic movie idol, though he was neither an Arab nor a Muslim. He was born Roman Catholic, of a French mother and an Italian father. But genealogy was not the point, nor was religion. The point was a dusky seducer of powder-white women. The point was a silken tent under the stars. The point was a theme for the junior prom. Like the Alhambra Theatre's architecture, Rudolf Valentino referred the American imagination to an indistinct kingdom somewhere between *A Thousand and One Nights* and the Old Testament.

For many older Americans, until 2001, Baghdad was a thought inseparable from Douglas Fairbanks.

In the big Bible movies, Arabs were supernumeraries, not yet Muslims. Arabs were sellers at the bazaars, tuggers of camels, blind beggars. Arabs were like the desert—shifty, enduring. Jews and Christians were the main players—buff, brown-nippled visionaries (Victor Mature) who suffered the twisted attentions of stuffed-togas (Peter Ustinov) or gold-sandaled sinners (Virginia Mayo).

Islam had no comparable fraudulent reality for me, not until *Lawrence of Arabia;* not until screenwriter Robert Bolt's desert princes (Omar Sharif, Alec Guinness) stung their camels' necks with batons, uttering exit lines such as "So it is written!" The princes were fatalistic foils to Peter O'Toole's blue-eyed "Nothing is written."

As an adolescent, I read Sir Richard Burton, the nineteenth-century English explorer, because he was there—a maroon half-leather volume on my favorite shelf at the public library ("Travels in Ancient Lands"). Burton smuggled me into Mecca beneath a filthy cloak—Mecca was forbidden to infidels—and he nearly got us killed by standing to urinate, something only an infidel would do. Burton said he knew that but thought no one was watching.

About the time of my hajj with Sir Richard Burton, two examples of Islam in America became apparent to me. When trickster-poet heavyweight champ Cassius Clay espoused the Nation of Islam, renaming himself Muhammad Ali, his conversion immediately drew the world's attention.

In parts of American cities, like Harlem, the South Side of Chicago, and East Oakland, the Nation of Islam was gaining notoriety as a Northern, an ultra-unorthodox, chapter of the Negro civil rights movement. Black Muslims dressed modestly—like Sunday school teachers, like Mormons, like nuns—but they preached what America feared more than integration: They preached separatism, puritanism, anti-Semitism, racial supremacy, a faith against other faiths, a faith against the United States. The Nation of Islam's claim on orthodox Islam was tenuous.

Muhammad Ali was a winner, the heavyweight boxing champion of the world, and, in his own words, a pretty man—a combination of attributes about as choice as anyone can claim in public America. Ali had more attributes still. A sly wit belied his ferocity in the ring. In his run-in with his draft board, Ali spoke with disarming moral authority. Many Americans, especially men of draft age, admired his refusal to fight in Vietnam. We saw in Ali not only a hero of physical culture, but an upstanding man— thoroughly, never obsequiously, an American. *("I ain't got no quarrel with them Viet Cong.")*

Like many of my generation, I became interested in another Black Muslim. There were no "Sweet-By-and-By" refrains in the testimony of Malcolm X. His voice was the puritan voice of the American North. Malcolm X had a strong story to tell of white racism and of his own degradation, but also of spiritual struggle and change.

I realize now there was always within my mother's *ojalá* the recognition that human lives are doomed to surprise. In 1973 I was a student living in London, a student walking through Hyde Park on a summer evening. My mother wrote in her weekly letter of a neighbor, whose fondest wish was to bring her grandchildren to Sacramento for the state fair, and whose leitmotif in my mother's correspondence was of perpetual reticence—to buy a cake or to play bingo or to go see *The Sound of Music*—because she was saving all her nickels and dimes to treat her grandchildren, etcetera. . . . Well, our friend did manage to bring most of her grandchildren into single file outside the turnstile one blistering August afternoon. As she waved the children forward with her fistful of tokens, she suddenly clutched at her bosom and fell down dead.

In 1964 Malcolm X separated himself from the Nation of Islam to become a Sunni Muslim. This was already a journey away from American provincialism. He traveled to the holy city of Mecca as a requirement of his faith, and he was astonished to meet all the tribes and kinds of people of the earth gathered there. It was in Mecca that Malcolm X found his spiritual inheritance—a vision larger than grievance, larger than America; a vision of belonging to the world and in the world.

Malcolm X was murdered in New York in 1965 as an apostate Black Muslim.

In the same letter, the fairground letter, as an aside, my mother mentioned that the Alhambra Theatre had closed. The property had been sold to Safeway.

At that time, Americans were daily reading about the Viet Cong and Ho Chi Minh in Hanoi and the labyrinthine Mekong Delta. We were abandoning the old downtowns of Amercian cities and their grandiose movie palaces. The theaters were boarded up or partitioned into two or three screens. In 1975 the last American helicopter lifted off from the besieged U.S. embassy in Saigon. Southeast Asian refugees began to arrive in California. By the time I returned to Sacramento, the Safeway Corporation had pulled down Samson's pillars. All that remained of the Alhambra Theatre was a tiled wall on the edge of a parking lot.

The new American movie theater, in the suburban mall, was a box, or several boxes, joined by a lobby of no romantic implication. Mall theaters did have the advantages of gigantic screens, rocking seats, free parking, and elaborate sound systems that could portray explosions and epic destructions with what we supposed was astonishing verisimilitude.

Among the many things we learned on the morning of September 11 was that epic destruction does not necessarily carry a sound in our memory or in our mind's eye.

# two

# Jerusalem and the Desert

On the flight from London I sit opposite a rumble seat where the stewardess places herself during takeoff. The stewardess is an Asian woman with a faraway look. I ask how often she makes this flight. Once or twice a month. Does she enjoy Israel? Not much. She stays in a hotel in Tel Aviv. She goes to the beach. She flies back. What about Jerusalem? She has not been there. What is in Jerusalem?

The illustrated guidebook shows a medieval map of the world. The map is round. The sun has a beard of fire. All the rivers of the world spew from the mouth of the moon. At the center of the world is Jerusalem.

Just inside the main doors of the Church of the Holy Sepulcher, tourists seem unsure how to respond to a rectangular slab of marble resting upon the floor. Lamps and censors and trinkets hang suspended above the stone. We watch as an old woman approaches. With some effort, she gets down on her knees. I flip through my book: *This marble represents the Stone of Unction where Jesus's body was anointed. This is not original; this stone dates from 1810.* The old woman bends forward to kiss the pale stone.

I have come to the Holy Land because the God of the Jews, the God of the Christians, the God of the Muslims—a common God—revealed Himself in this desert. My curiosity about an ecology that joins three religions dates from September 11, 2001, from prayers enunciated in the sky over America on that day.

Most occidental Christians are unmindful of the orientalism of Christianity. Over two millennia, the locus of Christianity shifted westward—to Antioch, to Rome, to Geneva, to the pale foreheads of Thomistic philosophers, to Renaissance paintings, to glitter among the frosts of English Christmas cards. Islam, too, in the middle centuries, swept into Europe with the Ottoman carpet, but then receded. (On September 11, 1683, the King of Poland halted the Muslim advance on Europe at the Gates of Vienna.) Only to reflux. Amsterdam, Paris are becoming Islamic cities.

After centuries of Diaspora, after the calamity of the Holocaust in Europe, Jews turned once more toward the desert. Zionists did not romanticize the desolate landscape. Rather, they defined nationhood as an act of planting. The impulse of the kibbutz movement remains the boast of urban Israel: to make the desert bloom.

The theme of Jerusalem is division. Friday. Saturday. Sunday. The city has been conquered, destroyed, rebuilt, garrisoned, halved, quartered, martyred, and exalted—always the object of spiritual desire, always the prize, always the corrupt model of the eventual city of God. The government of Ariel Sharon constructed a wall that separates Jerusalem from the desert, Jerusalem from Bethlehem, Easter from Christmas.

Jerusalem was the spiritual center of the Judean wilderness. It was Jerusalem the desert thought about. It was Jerusalem the prophets addressed. Jerusalem was where Solomon built a temple for the Lord and where God promised to dwell with His people. Jerusalem was where Jesus died and was resurrected. It was from Jerusalem that Muhammad ascended to heaven during his night journey.

My first impression of the city is my own loneliness—oil stains on the road, rubble from broken traffic barriers, exhaust from buses, the drift of cellophane bags. At the Damascus Gate an old woman sits on the pavement, sorting grape leaves into piles—or some kind of leaves. It is hot. Already it is hot. Late spring. It is early morning. There is a stench of uncollected garbage, and the cats, light and limp as empty purses, slink along the blackened stone walls. Shopkeepers are unrolling their shops.

I turn into the courtyard of the Church of the Holy Sepulcher, the site of Christ's burial and resurrection. A few paces away, within the church, is Golgotha, where Jesus was crucified. Golgotha, the Place of the Skull, is also, according to Jerusalem tradition, the grave of Adam. Jerusalem is as condensed, as self-referential, as Rubik's Cube.

I wait in line to enter the sepulcher, a freestanding chapel in the rotunda of the basilica. A mountain was chipped away from the burial cave, leaving only the cave. Later the cave was destroyed. What remains is the interior of the cave, which is nothing. The line advances slowly until, after two thousand years, it is my turn. I must lower my shoulders and bend my head; I must almost crawl to pass under the low opening.

I am inside the idea of the tomb of Christ.

I will return many times to the Church of the Holy Sepulcher during my stay and form in my mind an accommodation to its clamorous hush, to the musk of male asceticism—indeed, I will form a love for it that was not my first feeling. Though my first impression remains my last: emptiness.

I wait for Haim Berger in the lobby of a hotel in Ein Bokek, one among an oasis of resorts near the Dead Sea. The lobby is a desert of sand-colored marble. The lobby's temperature is oppressively beige; it would be impossible to cool this useless atrium. My cell phone rings. It is Maya, the director of the travel agency attached to my hotel in Jerusalem. Haim will be late one hour. Look for him at ten o'clock.

I watch a parade of elderly men and women crossing the lobby in bathing suits to catch a shuttle to the sulfur baths. They are so unself-conscious about their bodies they seem to walk in paradise.

I imagine I am waiting for someone in shorts and boots and aviator glasses, driving a Jeep. A Volkswagen pulls up and parks haphazardly.

A man bolts from the car. He is willowy of figure, dressed all in white, sandals, dark curly hair. He disappears into the hotel, reemerges. We wait side by side.

I cannot go to the desert alone. I am unfit for it. The desert requires a Jeep. It requires a hat and sunglasses and plastic liters of warm water it is no pleasure to drink. It requires a guide. It requires a cell phone.

Just now the man dressed in white begins patting his pockets, searching for his chiming cell. "*Ken . . . shalom*, Maya," I hear him say. Then, turning toward me, "Ah."

Haim Berger is full of apology. He has taken his wife to an emergency room. Yes, everything is all right. Just a precaution. There is an Evian bottle for me in the car. We will switch to the Jeep later.

Within ten minutes I am standing with Haim on the side of the highway. We look out over a plain, over what once was Sodom and Gomorrah. Haim asks if I know the story. Of course I know the story. Which, nevertheless, does not stop him from telling it. We might be standing near where Abraham stood when "Abraham saw dense smoke over the land, rising like fumes from a furnace." I ask Haim if he is religious. He is not.

All three desert religions claim Abraham as father. A recurrent question in my mind concerns the desert: Did Abraham happen upon God or did God happen upon Abraham? The same question: Which is the desert, or who? I came upon a passage in 2 Maccabees. The passage pertains to the holiness of Jerusalem: *The Lord, however, had not chosen the people for the sake of the Place, but the Place for the sake of the people.* So, God happened upon Abraham. Abraham is the desert.

An old man sits at the door of his tent in the heat of the day.

Between that sentence and this—within the drum of the hare's heart, within the dilation of the lizard's eye—God enters his creation. The old man, who is Abraham, becomes aware of three strangers standing nearby. They arrive without the preamble of distance. The nominative grammar of Genesis surpasses itself to reveal that one of these travelers is God or perhaps all three are God, like a song in three octaves. Abraham invites the Three to rest and to refresh themselves. In return, God promises that in a year's time Abraham's wife, who is long past childbearing, will hold in her arms a son.

Abraham's wife, Sarah, in the recesses of the tent, snorts upon hearing the prognostication; says, not quite to herself: Oh, sure!

God immediately turns to Abraham: *Why does Sarah laugh? Is anything too marvelous for God?*

Sarah says: I am not laughing.

God says: *Yes, you are.*

In 1947 a Bedouin goatherd lost a goat and climbed the side of a mountain to look for it. The boy entered a cave—today the cave is known worldwide among archaeologists as Qumran Cave 1. What the boy found in the cave—probably stumbled upon in the dark—were broken clay jars that contained five sheepskin scrolls.

Four of the scrolls were written in Hebrew, one in Aramaic. More scrolls were subsequently found by other Bedouin and by scholars in adjacent caves. The discovered scrolls—including a complete copy of the Book of Isaiah—are the oldest-known manuscript copies of books of the Bible.

The scrolls date to the second century BC. Scholars believe the Jewish sect of Essenes, of the proto-monastic community of Qumran, hid the texts we now know as the Dead Sea Scrolls. No one remembers whether the goatherd found his goat.

Haim is not religious but he offers to tell me a curious story: Last year he took a group of students into a mountainous part of the desert. He had been there many times. He had previously discovered markings on rocks that seemed to indicate religious observance; he believes the markings are ancient.

On the particular day he describes—it was the winter solstice—as the group approached a mountain, they saw what appeared to be a semicircle of flame emanating from the rock face, rather like the flame from a hoop in the circus. Haim knew it was a trick of the light, or perhaps gases escaping from a fissure in the rock. He walked before the mountain in an arc to observe the phenomenon from every angle. He repeats: He was not alone. They all saw it. He has photographs. He will show me the photographs.

Haim's love for the desert dates from his military service. His Jeep broke down one day. He cursed the engine. He slammed the hood. He took a memorable regard of the distance. Since that day, he has become intimate with the distance; he has come to see the desert as a comprehensible ecosystem that can be protective of humans.

Haim has tied a white kerchief over his hair.

Haim says: "Bedouin know a lot. Bedouin have lived in the

desert thousands of years." Haim says: "If you are ever stranded in the desert—*Are you listening to me? This may save your life!*—in the early morning, you must look to see in which direction the birds are flying. They will lead you to water."

Haim stops to speak with admiration of a bush with dry, gray-green leaves. "These leaves are edible." (Now I must sample them.) "They are salty, like potato chips." (They are salty.)

Of another bush: "These have water. If you crush them, you will get water. These could save your life." He crushes a fistful of leaves and tears spill from his hand.

The child of Abraham and Sarah is named Isaac, which means "He Laughs." Sarah proclaims an earthy Magnificat: *God has made laughter for me, and all who hear of it will laugh for me.* From the loins of these two deserts—Abraham, Sarah—God yanks a wet, an iri-descent, caul: a people as numerous as the stars. From the line of Sarah, royal David. From King David's line will come Jesus.

One's sense of elision begins with the map. Many tourist maps include the perimeters of the city at the time of Herod's temple, the time of Christ. *This once was . . . Built over the site . . . All that re-mains . . . This site resembles . . .*

*This is not the room of the Last Supper; this is a Crusader structure built over the room, later converted to a mosque—note the mihrab, the niche in the wall.*

The empty room is white—not white, golden. *Is the air really golden?* As a child in Omaha, my friend Ahuva was ravished by the thought—told her by an old man in a black hat—that the light of Jerusalem is golden. An ultra-Orthodox boy wanders into the room (a few paces from this room is the Tomb of King David, the anteroom to which is dense with the smell of men at prayer;

upstairs is a minaret); the boy is eating something, some kind of bun. He appears transfixed by a small group of evangelical Christian pilgrims who have begun to sing a song, what in America we would call an old song.

I am alone in the early morning at St. Anne's, a Romanesque church built in the twelfth century. The original church was damaged by the Persians; restored in the time of Charlemagne; destroyed, probably by the Caliph al-Hakim, in 1010. The present church was built by the Crusaders. Sultan Salah ad-Din captured the city in 1192 and converted the church to a madrassa. The Ottoman Turks neglected the structure; it fell to ruin. The Turks offered the church to France. The French order of White Fathers now administers St. Anne's. Desert sun pours through a window over the altar.

*Not only is the light golden, Ahuva, but I must mention a specific grace. Around four o'clock, the most delightful breeze comes upon Jerusalem, I suppose from the Mediterranean, miles away. It begins at the tops of the tallest trees, the date palm trees; shakes them like feather dusters; rides under the bellies of the lazy red hawks; snaps the flags on the consulate roofs; lifts the curtains of the tall windows of my room at the hotel—sheer curtains embroidered with an arabesque design—lifts them until they are suspended perpendicularly in midair like the veil of a bride tormented by a playful page, who then lets them fall. And then lifts. And then again.*

I walk around the wall of the city to the Mount of Olives, to a Christian sensibility the most evocative remnant of Jerusalem, for it matches—even including the garbage—one's imagination of Christ's regard for the city he approached from Bethany, which was from the desert. The desert begins immediately to the east of Jerusalem.

All the empty spaces of the Holy City—all courts, Tabernacles, tombs, and reliquaries—are resemblances and references to the emptiness of the desert. All the silences of women and men who proclaim the desert God throughout the world, throughout the ages, are references and resemblances to this—to the Holy City, to the hope of a Holy City. Jerusalem is the Bride of the Desert.

The desert prowls like a lion. I am fatigued from the heat, and I look about for some shade and a bottle of water. Having procured both at an outdoor stand (from a young man whose father kneels in prayer), I grow curious about an entrance I can see from the courtyard where I rest. Perhaps it is a chapel. An old man is sitting on the steps near the entrance. I approach him. What is this place?

"The Tomb of Mary," he answers.

Inside the door I perceive there are steps from wall to wall, leading downward. I can discern only the flickering of red lamps below, as if at the bottom of a well. When I reach the level of the tomb, an Orthodox priest throws a switch and the tomb is illuminated. It is a shelf of rock. The legend of the Dormition of Mary and the Catholic doctrine of the Assumption—neither of which I understand very well—lead me to wonder whether this is a spurious site. I decide I will accept all sites in this junk room of faith as true sites. I kneel.

A few years ago the bone box of James, the brother of Jesus, was raised from the shady world of the antiquities market. I believe the box has been discredited (dust not of the proper age within the incising of the letters). Authenticity is not my point. The stone box is my point. For it creates emptiness. Jerusalem is just such a box—within its anachronistic walls—a city of ossuaries, buried, reburied, hallowed, smashed, reconstructed, then called spurious or probable in guidebooks.

I have brought five guidebooks to Jerusalem: The Archeological. The Historical. The Illustrated. The Practical. The Self-Absorbed. Each afternoon, when I return to my hotel, I convene a colloquy among them—the chatter of guidebooks. I read one and then another.

The closed nature of the city frustrates my interest. My mind is oppressed by the inaccessibility of the hive of empty chambers, empty churches, empty tombs. The city that exists is superimposed in some meaty way over the bone city I long to enter. The streets are choked and impassible with life, the air stifling, the merchandise appalling. I feel feverish, but I think it is only the heat. I make the rounds of all the gates to the Temple Mount until at last I find the entrance that Israeli security will let me through—the passageway for infidels.

The sun is blazing on the courtyard. Even the faithful have gone away. Elsewhere the city is vertiginously sunken—resentments and miracles parfaited. Here there is a horizontal prospect.

The Al-Aqsa Mosque and the Dome of the Rock have been closed to non-Muslims since my last visit. I stand outside the shrine and try to reconstruct the interior from memory—the pillars, tiles, meadows of carpet. The vast Muslim space is what I remember. Islamic architecture attempts the sublime feat of emptiness. It is the sense of emptiness enclosed that is marvelous. The dome is the sky that is made. The sky is nothing—the real sky— and beggars have more of it than others.

Muslims own Jerusalem sky. This gold-leafed dome identifies Jerusalem on any postcard, the conspicuous jewel. Jews own the ground. The enshrined rock was the foundation for the Holy of Holies of Solomon's temple, the room that enclosed the Ark of the Covenant. The rock is also the traditional site of the near sacrifice of Isaac by Abraham. God commanded Moses to commission

Bezalel the artisan to make the ark. The Book of Exodus describes two golden cherubim whose wings were to form above the ark a Seat of Mercy—a space reserved for the presence of the Lord. The architecture for the presence of G-D has been conceptualized ever after as emptiness.

The paradox of monotheism is that the desert God, refuting all other gods, demands acknowledgment within emptiness. The paradox of monotheism is that there is no paradox—only unfathomable singularity.

*May I explain to you some features of the shrine?*

A man has approached as I stand gazing toward the dome. He looks to be in his sixties; he is neatly dressed in a worn suit. The formality of syntax extends to his demeanor. Obviously he is one of the hundreds of men, conversant in three faiths, who haunt the shrines of Jerusalem, hoping to earn something as informal guides.

No thank you.

*This is the Dome of the Rock,* he continues.

No thank you.

*Why are you so afraid to speak to a guide?* (The perfected, implicating question.)

I am not afraid. I don't have much time.

He lowers his eyes. *Perhaps another time.* He withdraws.

My diffidence is purely reflexive. One cannot pause for a moment on one's path through any of the crowded streets or souks without a young man—the son, the nephew, the son-in-law of some shopkeeper—asking, often with the courtliness of a prince, often with the stridency of a suitor: *May I show you my shop?*

Emptiness clings to these young men as well—the mermen of green-lit grottoes piled with cheap treasure—men with nothing to do but fiddle with their cell phones or yawn in their unconscious beauty and only occasionally swim up to someone caught in the unending tide of humanity that passes before them.

*May I show you my shop?*

No thank you.

To speak of the desert God is to risk blasphemy, because the God of the Jews and the Christians and the Muslims is unbounded by time or space, is everywhere present—exists as much in a high mountain village in sixteenth-century Mexico as in tomorrow's Jakarta, where Islam thrives as a tropical religion. Yet it was within the ecology of the Middle Eastern desert that the mystery of monotheism blazed. And it is the faith of the Abrahamic religions that the desert God penetrated time and revealed Himself first—thus condescending to sequence—to the Jews.

Behind the wall of my hotel in East Jerusalem are a gasoline station and a small mosque. The tower of the mosque—it is barely a tower—is outfitted with tubes of green neon. Five times in twenty-four hours the tubes of neon flicker and sizzle; the muezzin begins his cry. Our crier has the voice of an old man, a voice that gnaws on its beard. I ask everyone I meet if the voice is recorded or live. Some say recorded and some say real.

*I believe God is great. I believe God is greatest.*

The God of the Jews penetrated time. The Christian and the Muslim celebrated that fact ever after with noise. In the medieval town, Christian bells sounded the hours. Bells called the dawn and the noon and the coming night.

In the secular West, church bells have been stilled by discretion and by ordinance. In my neighborhood of San Francisco, the announcement of dawn comes from the groaning belly of a garbage truck.

No one at the hotel seems to pay the voice any mind. The waiters serve. Cocktails are shaken and poured. People in the court-yard and in the restaurant continue their conversations. The proprietress of the place turns a page of the book she is reading.

At four o'clock in the morning, the swimming pool is black. The hotel is asleep and dreaming. The neon ignites. The old man picks up his microphone to rend our dream asunder.

*It is better to pray than to sleep.*

The voice is not hectoring; it is simply oblivious. It is not like one's father, up early and dressing in the dark; it is like a selfish old man who can't sleep. The voice takes its permission from the desert—from the distance—but it is the modern city it wakes with enforced intimacy.

The old man's chant follows a tune; it is always the same tune, like a path worn through a carpet. And each day the old man becomes confused by the ornamental line—his voice is not agile enough to assay it. His voice turns ruminative, then puzzled. Finally, a nasal moan:

*Muhammad is the prophet of Allah.*

River Jordan water runs between my toes—a breathtakingly comfortable sensation. I have taken a bus tour of Galilee; the bus has stopped at the Yardenit Baptismal Site, which resembles a state picnic grounds. I watch a procession of Protestant pilgrims in rented white smocks descend some steps into the comfortable brown water.

Protestantism is the least oriental of the desert faiths. Protestants own little real estate within the walls of Jerusalem. They own nothing of ancient squabbles between the Holy Roman Empire, the Byzantine Empire, the Ottoman Empire. Protestants are free to memorialize sacred events without any compulsion to stand guard over mythic ground.

For example, the traditionally venerated site of Christ's baptism is near Jericho. After the Six-Day War in 1967, that location was declared off-limits to tourists. And so this place—Yardenit—of no historical or religious significance, was developed as a place to which Christians might come for baptism ceremonies. The faith of evangelical pilgrims at Yardenit overrides the commercialism that attaches to the enterprise (*Your Baptism videotaped by a professional*). One bank or the other, it is the same river, and pilgrims at Yardenit step confidently into the Bible.

Distance enters Abraham's seed with God's intimacy. A birth precedes the birth of Isaac. There is domestic strife of God's manufacture. For God also arranges that Sarah's Egyptian servant, Hagar, will bear Abraham a son. That son is Ishmael; the name means "He Listens." Sarah soon demands that Abraham send Hagar and her son away. *I cannot abide that woman. She mocks me.*

So Hagar and Ishmael are cast into the desert of Beersheba as Abraham and Sarah and the camels and tents and servants and flocks flow slowly away from them like a receding lake of dust.

Abruptly Haim tells me to stop. "Listen! The desert has a silence like no other," he says. "Do you hear a ringing in your ear? It is the bell of existence."

Not far from here, in Gaza, missiles are pitched through a blue sky. People who will be identified in news reports this evening as terrorists will shortly be killed or the innocent will be killed, people who even now are stirring pots with favored spoons or folding the last page of the morning paper to line the bird's cage.

I hear. What do I hear? I hear a truck shifting gears on a highway, miles away.

God hears the cry of Ishmael: God finds Hagar in the desert

and rescues her dying child by tapping a spring of water—a green silk scarf pulled from a snake hole. God promises Hagar that Ishmael, too, will be a nation. From Ishmael's line will come the Arab tribes, and from the Arab tribes, the Prophet Muhammad.

Mahdi, my Palestinian guide, pulls off the main road so I can see the Monastery of the Temptation in the distance. (Mahdi has been telling me about the years he lived in Riverside, California.) The monastery was built upon the mountain where Christ was tempted by Satan to consider the Kingdoms of the World. And here are we, tourists from the Kingdoms of the World, two thousand years later, regarding the mountain.

A figure approaches from the distance, surrounded by a nimbus of moisture. The figure is a Bedouin on foot. A young man but not a boy, as I first thought. He is very handsome, very thin, very small, utterly humorless. He extends, with his two hands, a skein of perhaps twenty-five bead necklaces. He speaks English— a few words like beads. "Camel," he says. "For your wife, your girlfriend."

"This is camel," he says again, fingering some elongated beads. I ask him who made the necklaces. His mother.

There is no sentimentality to this encounter. Sentimentality is an expenditure of moisture. The Bedouin's beseeching eyes are dry; they are the practice of centuries. He sits down a short distance away from us while we contemplate the monastery. He looks into the distance, and, as he does so, he becomes the desert.

Moses, Jesus, Muhammad—each ran afoul of cities: Moses of the court of Egypt, Jesus of Jerusalem, Muhammad of Mecca. The desert hid them, emptied them, came to represent a period of trial before they emerged as vessels of revelation. Did they, any of them, experience the desert as habitable—I mean, in the manner of Haim, in the manner of the Bedouin?

After he fled Egypt, Moses took a wife; he took the nomadic life of his wife's people as a disguise. Moses led his father-in-law's flock across the desert to Mount Horeb, where God waited for him.

As a boy, Muhammad crossed the desert in Meccan caravans with his uncle Abu Talib. Muhammad acquired the language of the Bedouin and Bedouin ways. As a middle-aged man, Muhammad was accustomed to retire with his family to a cave in the desert to meditate. During one such retreat Muhammad was addressed by God.

The Jews became a people by the will of God, for He drove them through the desert for forty years. God fed the people Israel with manna. Ravens fed Elijah during his forty days in the desert. After his ordeal of forty days, Jesus accepted the ministrations of angels. Such supernatural nourishments of the body suggest a reliance on God rather than an embrace of the desert.

In *The Desert Fathers,* Helen Waddell writes that the early Christian monks of the desert gave a single intellectual concept to Europe—eternity. The desert monks saw the life of the body as "most brief and poor." But the life of the spirit lies beyond the light of day. The light of day conceals "a starlit darkness into which a man steps and becomes suddenly aware of a whole universe, except that part of it which is beneath his feet."

There are people in every age who come early or late to a sense of the futility of the world. Some people, such as the monks of the desert, flee the entanglements of the world to rush toward eternity. But even for those who remain in the world, the approach of eternity is implacable. "The glacier knocks in the cupboard, / The desert sighs in the bed," was W. H. Auden's mock-prophetic forecast. He meant the desert is incipient in the human condition. Time melts away from us. Even in luxuriant weather, even in luxuriant wealth, even in luxuriant youth, we know our bodies will fail; our buildings will fall to ruin.

If the desert beckons the solitary, it also, inevitably, gives birth to the tribe. The ecology of the desert requires that humans form communities for mutual protection from extreme weathers, from bandits, from rival chieftains. Warfare among Arab tribes impinged often upon the life of the Prophet Muhammad. In response to the tyranny of kinship, Muhammad preached a spiritual brotherhood—discipleship under Allah—that was as binding as blood, as expansive as sky.

The Christian monastic movement in the Judaean wilderness reached its peak in the sixth century, by which time there were so many monks, so many monasteries in the desert (as many as eight hundred monks in some of the larger communities), that it became a commonplace of monastic chronicles, a monkish conceit, to describe the desert as a city.

I am driving with Mahdi through Bethlehem, then several Bedouin settlements to the east, leading into the desert. The road narrows, climbs, eventually runs out at the gates of Mar Saba, a Greek Orthodox monastery.

A monk opens the gate. Mahdi asks in Arabic if we may see the monastery. The monk asks where we are from. The monk then takes up a metal bar, which he clangs within a cast-iron triangle.

Waiting in the courtyard below is another monk. He greets us in English. Obviously four bangs, or however many, on the contraption upstairs summons English. The monk's accent is American. He, too, asks where I am from. He is from St. Louis.

We are first shown the main church. The church is dark, complexly vaulted, vividly painted. We are told something of the life of Saint Saba, or Sabas, the founder of the monastery. Saba died in AD 532. "He is here," the monk then says, ushering us to a glass case in a dark alcove, where the saint lies in repose. "The remains are uncorrupted."

The monk carries a pocket flashlight that he shines on the corpse of the saint. The thin beam of light travels up and down the body; the movement of the light suggests sanctification by censing. The figure is small, leathern, clothed in vestments. This showing takes place slowly, silently—as someone would show you something of great importance in a dream.

We ask about another case, the one filled with skulls. They are the skulls of monks killed by Persians in AD 614. One has the impression the young monk considers himself to be brother to these skulls, that they remain a part of the community of Mar Saba, though no longer in the flesh. One has the impression grievance endures.

The monk next leads us to the visitors' parlor. No women are allowed in the monastery. In this room the masculine sensibility of the place has unconsciously re-created a mother's kitchen. The monk disappears into a galley; he returns with a repast that might have been dreamed up by ravens: tall glasses of lemonade, small glasses of ouzo, a plate of chocolates. The lemonade is very cool, and we ask how this can be without electricity. Butane, the monk answers. For cooking and refrigeration.

The monk's patience is for the time when we will leave. Until this: "What has brought you to the Holy Land?"

I have come to write about the desert religions, I reply. I am interested in the fact that three great monotheistic religions were experienced within this ecology.

"Desert religions, desert religions," the monk repeats. Then he says: "You must be very careful when you use such an expression. It seems to equate these religions."

I do mean to imply a common link through the desert.

"Islam is a perversion," he says.

A few minutes later, the monk once more escorts us through the courtyard to the stone steps. He shakes my hand and says what I remember as conciliatory, though it may not have been: "The desert creates warriors."

Haim makes his living conducting tours of the desert. He is, as well, a student and an instructor at Ben-Gurion University of the Negev, where we stop briefly to exchange vehicles.

Haim invites me into his house; he must get some things. Haim's wife is also a graduate student at the university. There are some pleasant drawings of dancers on the walls. The curtains are closed against the desert. Mrs. Berger returns while I am waiting. She is attractive, blond, pregnant, calm. "You turned on the air-conditioning," she says to Haim—not accusatorily but as a statement of (I assume unusual) fact. "I have to gather some things," he replies. I ask if I may see the photograph of the mountain.

"Ah, Haim's mountain." Mrs. Berger conveys affection, indulgence.

Haim goes to his computer, pulls up the images: the mountain from the distance. Closer. Closer. The suggestion of a rectangular shape. I hesitate to say the shape of tablets; nevertheless, that is how it appears. It is difficult to ascertain the scale. Yes, I can see—along the top and side of the rectangular shape there are what appear to be flames.

Haim carries several filled grocery bags out to the Jeep. We leave Mrs. Berger standing in the dark kitchen. *Goodbye.*

Stephen Pfann looks to be in his forties. His hair is white; he wears a beard. He has large pale eyes of the sort one sees in Victorian photographs. It is because of his resemblance, in my imagination, to a Victorian photograph that I attribute to him the broad spirit of Victorian inquiry. Stephen's discourse has a dense thread count, weaving archaeology, geology, history, theology, also botany and biology. Stephen's teenage children seem adept at reining him in when he is kiting too high. He and his wife, Claire, administer the University of the Holy Land, a postgraduate biblical institute in Jerusalem. Stephen says he would be willing to take me to Qumran. He suggests an early morning expedition and promises, as well, an Essene liturgy at sunrise.

My imagination runs away: prayers within a cave. Clay lamps, shadows. Some esotericism in the liturgy and a sun like the sound of a gong.

On the appointed morning, Stephen picks me up at my hotel. As it is already bone-light, I presume we have missed the sunrise. But, in fact, we are reciting psalms on a level plain beneath Cave 1 as the sun comes up over Arabia, over Jordan, over the Dead Sea. The light is diffuse, though golden enough. The texts remark the immensity of creation. (I am thinking about a movie I saw. An old man—Omar Sharif—whispers as he dies: "I am going to join . . . the immensity.")

We have been joined here by several others, two Pfann children and a forensic pathologist connected with the University of the Holy Land.

Stephen mentions "the umbilicus," by which term he means the concentration of God's intention on this patch of earth. Underfoot is a large anthill—a megalopolis—then a satellite colony, then another, then another, the pattern extending across the desert floor.

*The old woman bends forward to kiss the pale stone.*

We begin our climb to Cave 1. The air has warmed. Stephen Pfann, in his stride, points at minute flora; his daughter nods and photographs them. He and his children are as nimble as goats. "Is everyone all right?" Pfann calls downward.

I am not all right. I am relegated at several junctures to using both hands and feet. The good-natured pathologist climbing ahead of me is watchful and discreet with his helping hand, all the while recounting the religious conversion that brought him to the Holy Land.

The cave is not cool, by the way. A smell of bat dung. I hear Stephen saying something about the rapidity of the transfer of heat molecules from one substance to another. (The dryness of the cave preserved the scrolls.) I am perspiring. I am making toe marks in the dust.

Hundreds of thousands of years ago, water receded from this cave. Two thousand years ago, an Essene—probably an Essene—filled a basket with grating clay jars and climbed to this cave to hide the holy scrolls against some intimation of destruction. Sixty years ago, a Bedouin goatherd, muttering goat curses—an old man now if he survives—came upon five clay vats spilling revelation.

The community of Qumran was destroyed by Roman legions in AD 68.


Dogma strives to resemble the desert: It is dry; it is immovable. Truth does not change. Is there something in the revelation of God that retains—because it has passed through—properties of desert or maleness or Semitic tongue? Does the desert, in short, make warriors? That is the question I bring to the desert from the twenty-first century.

The Semitic God is the God who enters history. Humans

examine every event that pertains to us for meaning. The motive of God who has penetrated time tempts us to imperfect conjecture. When armies are victorious, when armies are trodden in the dust, when crops fail, when volcanoes erupt, when seas drink multitudes, it must mean God intends it so. What did we do to deserve this? King David psalmed for the vanquishing of his enemies, did he not? There is something in the leveling jealousy of the desert God that summons a possessive response in us. *We are His people* becomes *He is our God*. The blasphemy that attaches to monotheism is the blasphemy of certainty. If God is on our side, we must be right. We are right because we believe in God. We must defend God against the godless. Certitude clears a way for violence. And so the monk's dictum—the desert creates warriors—can represent centuries of holy war and sordid prayer and an umbilicus that whips like a whirlwind.

In Afghanistan's central plateau there were two mountain-high Buddhas. For centuries, caravans traveling the Silk Route would mark them from miles away. The Bamiyan Buddhas were destroyed by the Taliban in 2001; their faces are now anvils, erasures. An inscription from the Koran was painted beside the alcove of the larger Buddha: *The just replaces the unjust.* Just so do men destroy what belief has built, and they do it in the name of God, the God who revealed Himself in the desert, the desert that cherishes no monuments, wants none. *There is no God but God.*

On July 16, 1945, the first nuclear weapon was tested in the American desert. The ape in our hearts stood still. Wow.

*The desert creates warriors*, by which construction Saint Sabas meant (for it was his construction) that the monk discerns his true nature in the desert—his true nature in relation to God—and the discernment entails learning to confront and to overcome the temptations of human nature. In that sense, a warrior.

*The desert creates lovers.* Saint Sabas desired the taste of an apple. The craving was sweeter to him than the thought of God. From that moment Sabas foreswore apples. The desire for apples was the taste of God.

Desert is the fossil of water. (Haim has been at great pains to point this out—striations in mesas and the caverns water has bored through mountains of salt, and salt is itself a memory of water.) Is dogma a fossil of the living God—the shell of God's passage—but God is otherwise or opposite? Perhaps it is that the Semitic tongues are themselves deserts—dry records of some ancient fluency, of something feminine that has withdrawn. The Semitic tongues descend from Shem, son of Noah, survivor of the Flood. Abraham was of Shem's line. Perhaps the Semitic tongues, inflected in the throat, recall water.

I have often heard it observed by critics of the desert religions that monotheism would have encouraged in humankind a more tender relationship to nature if the Abrahamic God had revealed Himself from within a cloak of green. The desert encourages a sense of rebuff and contest with the natural world. Jesus cursed the recalcitrant fig tree right down to firewood.

The desert's uninhabitability convinces Jew and Christian and Muslim that we are meant for another place. Within the deserts of the Bible and the Koran, descriptions of Eden, descriptions of the Promised Land, resemble oases. For Jews, Eden was pre-desert. For Christians and Muslims, paradise—reconciliation with God—is post-desert.

In the Koran, paradise is likened to gardens underneath which rivers flow. For Christians, paradise is an urban idea, a communion, the city of God. The commendation of the body in the ancient rite of Christian burial prays that angels may come to lead the soul of the departed to the gates of the holy city Jerusalem.

I purchase for five shekels a postcard scene of Jerusalem in the snow—black-and-white—the sky is dark but Jerusalem shines swan, a royal city. I will show you the photograph.

I follow Haim a quarter of a mile to a grove of untrimmed date palm trees. I have seen their like only in ancient mosaics, the muted colors, the golden dust. In their undressed exuberance these palms resemble fountains. But they are dry; they prick and rattle as we thread our way among them. We could just as easily have walked around, couldn't we? I suspect Haim of concocting an oasis experience. But his glance is upward, into the branches of some taller trees. Haim is hoping for what he calls a lucky day. If it is Haim's lucky day, we will see a leopard. Recently, a leopard entered the town of Beersheba. Haim suspects the creature may be lurking here.

But it is not Haim's lucky day. We continue up an incline, alongside a muddy riverbed. Winged insects bedevil my ears. We walk around a screen of acacia trees, at which Haim steps aside to reveal . . . a waterfall, a crater filled with green water! There are several Israeli teenagers swimming, screaming with delight as they splash one another. A tall African youth stands poised at the edge of the pool.

This Ethiopian Jew (we later learn) has come to this desert from another. He has come because the Abrahamic faith traveled like particles of desert over mountains and seas, blew under the gates of ancient cities, and caught in the leaves of books. Laughter, as spontaneous as that of his ancestress Sarah, echoes through the canyon as the boy plunges into the stone bowl of water. Displaced water leaps like a javelin.

I am standing in the Negev desert. I am wet.

John the Baptist wrapped himself in camel hide. He wandered the desert and ate the desert—honey and locusts and Haim's gray leaves. John preached hellfire and he performed dunking ceremonies in the river Jordan. People came from far and wide to be addressed by the interesting wild man as "Brood of Vipers." When watery Jesus approached flaming John and asked for baptism, John recognized Jesus as greater than he. It was as though the desert bowed to the sea. But, in fact, their meeting was an inversion of elements. John said: *I baptize only with water. The one who comes after me will baptize with Spirit and fire.*

Desert is, literally, emptiness—its synonyms "desolation," "wasteland." To travel to the desert "in order to see it," in order to experience it, is paradoxical. The desert remains an absence. The desert is this empty place I stand multiplied by infinite numbers—

not this place particularly. So I come away each night convinced I have been to the holy desert (and have been humiliated by it) and that I have not been to the desert at all.

Just beyond the ravine is a kibbutz, a banana plantation, a university, a nuclear power plant. But, you see, I wouldn't know that. The lonely paths Haim knows are not roads. They are scrapings of the earth. Perhaps they are tracks that Abraham knew, or Jesus. Some boulders have been removed and laid aside. From the air-conditioned van or from the tossing Jeep or through binoculars, I see the desert in every direction. The colors of the desert are white, fawn, tawny gold, rust, rust-red, blue. When the ignition is turned off and the Jeep rolls to a stop, I pull the cord that replaces the door handle; the furnace opens; my foot finds the desert floor. But the desert is distance. Nothing touches me.

Yet many nights I return to my hotel with the desert on my shoes. There is a burnt, mineral scent in my clothing. The scent is difficult to wash out in the bathroom basin, as is the stain of the desert, an umber stain.

Standing, scrubbing my T-shirt, is the closest I get to the desert. The water turns yellow.

I tell myself I am not looking for God. I am looking for an elision that is, nevertheless, a contour. The last great emptiness in Jerusalem is the first. What remains to be venerated is the Western Wall, the ancient restraining wall of the destroyed Second Temple.

After the Six-Day War, the Israeli government bulldozed an Arab neighborhood to create Western Wall Plaza, an emptiness to facilitate devotion within emptiness—a desert that is also a well.

I stand at the edge of the plaza with Magen Broshi, a distinguished archaeologist. Magen is a man made entirely of Jerusalem. You can't tell him anything. Last night at dinner in the hotel garden, I tried out a few assertions I thought dazzling, only to be met with Magen's peremptory *Of course.*

Piety, ache, jubilation, many, many classes of ardor pass us by. Magen says he is not a believer. I tell Magen about my recent cancer. If I asked him, would he pray for me here, even though he does not believe? *Of course.*

Western Wall Plaza levels sorrow, ecstasy, cancer, belief. Here emptiness rises to proclaim its unlikeness to God, who allows for no comparison. Emptiness does not resemble. It is all that remains.

"No writing! You cannot write here." A woman standing nearby has noticed I carry a notebook. I have a pen in my hand. The woman means on the Sabbath, I think. Or can one never write here? It is the Sabbath.

"He is not writing anything," Magen mutters irritably, waving the woman away.

# three

## The True Cross

*A little water and the desert breaks into flower, bowers of cool shade spring up in the midst of dust and glare, radiant stretches of soft colour gleam in that grey expanse. Your heart leaps as you pass through the gateway in the mud wall; so sharp is the contrast, that you may stand with one foot in an arid wilderness and the other in a shadowy, flowery paradise.*

—Gertrude Bell, *Persian Pictures*

A sixty-nine-year-old body is still beautiful. It refuses any covering. A nurse is standing by the bed when we walk in. The nurse attempts to drape the genitals of the man on the bed with the edge of the sheet. But the hand of the man on the bed plucks the sheet away.

I'm afraid modesty is out the window, the nurse says.

There are two large windows.

There are three chairs for visitors, comfortable chairs; there is a foldout sofa for a spouse—that would be Peter, Luther's partner of thirty years, more than thirty years. Peter called two days ago. He said it was time.

So Jimmy and I drove to Las Vegas on Holy Thursday. Luther has been Jimmy's friend for more than forty years. They met when they were both shoe-leather messengers at a law firm in San Francisco; that was before FedEx, before fax, before e-mail. In those days the windows of the nineteenth floor of the Standard Oil Building could be opened to the hum of traffic below; "Proud

Mary," KFRC-AM Top Forty toiled through the speaker of a transistor radio on the windowsill behind the dispatcher's desk.

Peter hasn't slept properly for weeks. He tells me he shoves the couch against the bed at night so he can hold on to Luther's hand.

One time, when Luther had to go home to South Carolina on family business, Jimmy went with him. They walked through the woods behind the house where Luther had grown up. Luther pointed to a branch distended over a brown creek. *The old people used to tell us Jesus's cross was made of yonder tree. Every Easter, the tree puts out white blossoms by way of apology.*

The body on the bed slowly turns. Bares its teeth. Luther is smiling. Luther wants to tell Jimmy something right away. He motions with his hand: *Mama came to me a few days ago. She said it wasn't time yet.*

One time, Luther's Mama woke up in the middle of the night and there was this old man sitting on her bed. You go away, she said to the old man.

*Weren't you scared, Mama?*

No, not especially, but I didn't like it.

*Maybe you were asleep.*

No, sir, I wasn't.

*Well, what'd he do?*

He just sat there staring at the floor like he was waiting for further instructions. You go away right now, I told him; I clapped my hands at him like I was a cross little schoolteacher, and I pulled the covers up over my head and said my prayers.

*Who was it, Mama?*

I don't know who it was; I pulled up the covers and said my prayers. He went away and he never came back.

Mama died more than ten years ago.

The desk clerk at the Bellagio upgrades us to a suite—large, but not as commodious as Luther's room at the Nathan Adelson Hospice on North Buffalo Drive. The view from Luther's room is of the parking lot of a small business park. A placard on the wall next to the window cautions hospice visitors to park only in designated slots.

At the Bellagio, our room overlooks the hotel's six-acre lake, an allusion to Lago di Como. The Bellagio's lake has an advantage over its inspiration: At fifteen-minute intervals, jets of water are witched up into the air by a Frank Sinatra–Billy May rendition of Frank Loesser's "Luck Be a Lady." The jets shimmy, they fan, they collapse with a splat when the hydraulic pressure deserts them. Beyond Lago di Como, we can just see the tip of the Eiffel Tower.

In 1955 the management of Wilbur Clark's Desert Inn invited Nöel Coward, the British playwright and composer, to perform a cabaret act in Las Vegas.

Coward rather imagined he might end up tap-dancing to tommy-gun fire, so prevalent was the Vegas association with gangland. But he was agog at the money offered—thirty grand a week—at a time when his career was in a slump. (Coward had been superseded on the London stage by a new generation of playwrights; there wasn't much call in the West End or on Broadway for brittle drollery.) But then, Nöel Coward was a legend, and Las Vegas, because it was on the make, preferred legends.

Stars who might be on the downward slope of Hollywood or New York can achieve tenure in Las Vegas if they deliver what is remembered. Coward fit the bill. Frank Sinatra, Wayne Newton, Liberace, Cher, Debbie Reynolds, Tom Jones, Charo, Mitzi Gaynor,

Céline Dion, Bette Midler, Patti Page—the golden legends of the Strip are as odd as you please, but Las Vegas audiences (as used to be the case in London and Paris, and perhaps still is) have long, fond memories.

Upon his arrival, Coward wrote colleagues in London: "The gangsters who run the places are all urbane and charming." During the course of Coward's run, *Life* magazine photographer Loomis Dean rented a Cadillac limousine, stocked it with ice and liquor, and drove Coward fifteen miles into the desert to photograph him taking a cup of tea in the wilderness, attired in what Coward described as "deep evening dress." The photographer used the desert as the geographical equivalent of a straight man. The famous photographs perfectly captured the incongruous equipoise that describes the Vegas aesthetic.

Forty years ago, more than forty years, my friend Marilyn announced she was going to Las Vegas to see Elvis Presley. "Come," she said. "You have to see Las Vegas at least once before you die," she said.

We drove through a summer night. Sheet lightning blinked in the eastern sky. I listened as Marilyn described her father's gambling addiction—how he never lost a gentleman's amiability at the gaming table, how he had squandered most of his mother's fortune.

The Las Vegas hospitality industry is understandably respectful of losers. Marilyn's father never paid for a hotel room in Las Vegas, or for a meal or a drink. The city's generosity extended to the good loser's next of kin. All Marilyn needed to do was to phone her father, who, in turn, phoned the general manager of the Flamingo Hotel. The Flamingo comped us in what I guess you would call the wink of an eye.

In the morning, Marilyn passed her name to the Flamingo concierge, declaring we had come to see Elvis at the International. Elvis at the International was sold-out for the entire run. The concierge picked up the phone, called a uniformed officer of comparable rank at the International. And it was done. The only question that devolved to Marilyn and me was how much to tip the headwaiter at the International.

Elvis Presley first came to Las Vegas in 1956, when he was twenty-one years old. Middle-aged audiences in Las Vegas heard him with interested puzzlement at that time. Elvis was fresh—he was certainly famous—but he displayed none of that finger-snapping, syringe-in-the-toilet, up-tempo flash that Vegas found so inebriating. In 1969, on his return, Presley was nearer in age to the women in the audience, and he had learned the Vegas sell.

The messenger room at the law firm in San Francisco was like a prison movie—time measured in poker games, crossword puzzles, knives, novels. A never-neatened splatter of *Playboy* magazines on a junked conference table. Perpetual "Proud Mary." One corner of the room supported a mountain of legal briefcases. Another corner was a parking lot for dollies. There were fifteen messengers who sat on fifteen oaken office chairs facing the dispatcher, as in a minstrel show. When a messenger returned from a hike, his name was added to the bottom of the list; he sat down. (Messengers must be male. No experience necessary.) When a messenger took a hike, his name was crossed off the top of the list.

Luther got into the habit of stopping by a senior partner's office every afternoon for a chat, as if they were two free citizens of Athens. Luther found the Old Man interesting—his stories of growing up in turn-of-the-century California, of riding his pony over golden hills, of boarding a train that took him away to Harvard College, of homesickness, of scarlet fever. "Well, that's how I learned self-reliance," the Old Man said.

The Old Man was interested in Luther, too. Luther had gumption. Luther had learned self-reliance from his mother, who worked in a chicken-processing plant, who raised ten children, whose husband left.

Where's Luther? The dispatcher ran his finger down the list of scratched-out names. Proud Mary, *unh, unh*. Luther was in the Old Man's office, everyone knew.

One day, after Luther had been working for the law firm for a year, he told the Old Man he figured it was about time he tried something else.

Like what?

Like working for the phone company. The Old Man grabbed up his telephone and barked "TelCo" to his secretary, which was short for: Please get me the president of the telephone company.

Once the president of the telephone company had been procured for him (the firm represented every major California utility), the Old Man hollered into the receiver, as if from the bridge of his yacht: "Look, F., I have a young man here desirous of a career change. I'm going to send him over. Whom should he ask for? Sears as in catalog? Good-o! Love to Dotty."

Luther went for his appointment at the phone company. He wore the black suit that he and Andrew and Jimmy shared. The suit belonged to Luther, but they all wore it—Andrew to be a pallbearer, Jimmy to be best man, Andrew to the opera, Luther to apply for a job at the phone company.

Right off, the employment manager offered Luther a job as a messenger. Luther pivoted on his heel, walked back to the law firm, elevator to the nineteenth, straight into the Old Man's office. Messengers didn't have to knock. Luther stood facing the Old

Man. With a shamed and thumping heart, Luther said: *If I wanted to be a messenger, I could have stayed right here.*

The Old Man didn't get it right away, that Luther had been offered the job he already had. Once he did understand, the Old Man seized the phone with relish, catching the scent of hare. "Now look here," the Old Man's voice rolled like thunder over Mr. Sears's salutation. "I meant for the kid I sent to get a leg up. He's already a messenger. Why would you offer him a job as a messenger? I'm going to send him back, and I expect you to offer him a decent job."

The Old Man slammed down the telephone and winked at Luther: "Off you go, kid."

The following week, Luther began training in the switch room of the telephone company. Over the years, he worked himself into the highest classification of every job he was assigned; he moved from switchman to trunk man to optical-fiber cable work. (The Old Man died.) To something so specialized he was one of only two or three technicians who knew how to do whatever it was he did.

The joke among the three friends was: Who gets to be buried in the black suit? And what will the mourners wear?

We establish a little routine. Twice a day I commute between the hospice on North Buffalo and the Bellagio on Las Vegas Boulevard South. Drop Jimmy off in the morning, spend a couple of hours at the hospice, pick Jimmy up in the late afternoon. In between, I look around. There is a street in town named Virgil. The famous hotels on the Strip are not actually located in Las Vegas, but in an unincorporated entity called Paradise.

In the nineteenth century, Rafael Rivera, a Spanish scout—a teenager—joined a trading exploration party out of New Mexico that sought to establish a new trail to Los Angeles. Their hope was to find fresh water along the way. The party left Abiquiú in November of 1829. Rivera separated from the group at the Colorado River junction. He was, as far as anyone knows, the first European to enter the valley, to find the two lucky springs there, or, at any rate, to infer water from the vegetation of the valley. Rivera named the oasis Las Vegas—"the Meadows."

The main street downtown is named for John Charles Frémont. In 1844 Frémont led a surveying expedition that followed the San Joaquin River south, through the long Central Valley of California. At the Mojave River, Frémont's party veered eastward, crossed the Sierra, then followed the Old Spanish Trail for a time. Las Vegas was already a place of refreshment along the Spanish Trail, a trail that had been blazed more than a decade earlier by Rafael Rivera. Frémont recorded two streams of clear water: "The taste of the water is good, but rather warm to be agreeable." The streams, however, "afforded a delightful bathing place."

John Frémont died of peritonitis in a boardinghouse in New York City on July 13, 1890. No one I talk to can tell me what happened to Rafael Rivera; whether he returned to New Mexico or Old Mexico or Spain; whether he married; where he lies buried.

Recently, a complex of hotels and condos and offices in a sober international style has opened on the Strip under the mundane designation CityCenter. Its owners obviously intend a kind of restraint Las Vegas normally does not engage—gray exteriors, dark atriums. The visitor could be in São Paulo or Seoul or wherever the money flies. A cab driver tells me the new complex will not draw because there is no craziness to it. Here, you gotta be crazy, he says. Togas. Tigers. Tits.

In the lobby of the Aria hotel, part of the CityCenter complex, an eighty-four-foot-long sculpture, *Silver River*, by Maya Lin, is suspended behind the registration desk like a bough. Credit cards click across the marble counter as hotel guests check in or out. Maya Lin's sculpture is a trace-image of the Colorado River; it was cast from thirty-seven hundred pounds of "reclaimed" silver—sauceboats and Saint Christopher medals. The sculpture resembles artery, lightning, umbilicus, statistical graph.

During the week we are in town, there is a competition in Las Vegas among investors who are interested in developing a gangland museum. (And, two years later—Valentine's Day, 2012—the $42 million Mob Museum has opened.)

Other American cities might prefer to forget a criminal past. Las Vegas foresees profit in promoting its dark legend as an invitation to middle-class visitors to risk a little carelessness—to gamble more than they should, to tip the topless waitress more than necessary. Compared with Berlin in the thirties, compared with Ciudad Juárez today, compared with nineteenth-century America of the robber barons, compared with Chicago of the twenties, compared with Wall Street, "Sin City" must seem a wader's pool of wickedness. The sin on show is not what would be unimaginable in Indianapolis. Rather, it is precisely what Indianapolis would come up with if Indianapolis were charged with imagining Sin City.

On the grounds of the Flamingo Hotel, over by the wedding chapel, stands a monument to the mobster Benjamin "Bugsy" Siegel. Hollywood mythmakers credit Siegel with the idea of Las Vegas. Siegel's idea of Las Vegas was the idea of luxury and chance in a landscape where there was no chance of luxury.

Benjamin Siegel was born in 1906 to Russian immigrant parents in the Williamsburg section of Brooklyn, New York. He constructed his sense of glamour—of class, I think he would have said—against the meanness of the streets of his childhood and the distant Manhattan skyline. According to *Bugsy*, the 1991 Barry Levinson movie, Las Vegas was a sandlot prior to Siegel's coming. In truth, by the time Siegel conceived the potential for money in Las Vegas, there were already hotels and gambling parlors downtown, along Fremont Street. And the El Rancho Vegas had opened in 1941 on the two-lane highway that would later become the Strip—six years before Siegel's Flamingo.

What Siegel conceived was an aesthetic, and a pretty good one: He intended to build a resort in a desert-moderne style—something along the lines of Frank Lloyd Wright, something along the lines of Palm Springs—a lure for the best class of people, by which Siegel meant Hollywood. L.A. likes to think of Las Vegas as the populuxe mirage of Hollywood, a place where middle-class tourists look like movie stars but aren't, spend like millionaires but aren't.

Siegel went overbudget constructing his dream and the fancy people didn't show. Mobsters were looking at a loss. Benjamin Siegel was shot in the head in Beverly Hills, California, on June 20, 1947. He is buried in the Hollywood Forever Cemetery, Hollywood, California.

No sooner had Peter left to make some phone calls and to try to take a nap than Luther turned his head toward Jimmy: *Bathroom*.

I'll tell the nurse, said Jimmy.

*Hurry*, Luther said.

Jimmy hurried. The nurse was at her station. Mr. Thomas needs to make a bowel movement, Jimmy reported. The nurse turned from her computer, paused, as if she were about to say something wonderfully unhelpful. Instead, she said: OK, I'll talk to him.

Mr. Thomas, the nurse said, coming into his room.

*Bathroom*, said Luther. (Bambi.)

You are too weak to get to the bathroom, Mr. Thomas. There is a plastic towel underneath you—she gave the towel a tug. You can have a bowel movement right where you are. Press the buzzer if you need me. The nurse placed another half-plastic, half-paper sheet over Luther's midriff. She glanced at the thermostat. She left the room.

Luther turned toward Jimmy, removed the sheet, smiled. *Bandage*, said Luther.

There is no way Jimmy is afraid of Luther—Morphine Luther, Luther Demented, Luther with one foot in the grave. But this, Jimmy saw, was play.

Bandage? Jimmy said.

Luther grabbed the aluminum bed gate and rolled himself onto his right shoulder. Now Jimmy could see Luther's backside was papered over with a disc of green latex.

*Off*, said Luther.

Jimmy examined the bandage. (Probably a bedsore.) What's that for?

*Off*, said Luther. (The Red Queen.) Luther came late to the literature of childhood. In his thirties he read nursery classics. He loved them. The Alice books. *The Rescuers*. *Winnie-the-Pooh*.

I'll ask the nurse, said Jimmy.

Excuse me, he said. Again. I'm sorry but Mr. Thomas cannot have a bowel movement because there is a bandage covering his bottom, Jimmy reported to the nurse at her station.

If you press the button, someone will come, said the nurse at her station. The bandage will not hinder Mr. Thomas, she added.

Jimmy returned to the room to tell Luther he could have a bowel movement with a green latex waffle pasted to his behind. The game had progressed in his absence.

*Chair,* smiled Luther, his purse-arm extended vaguely. (Mrs. Miniver.)

You want to sit for a while?

*Down.* Luther indicated the bed gate. Jimmy crouched to examine the lever of the bed gate, then finally succeeded in lowering it.

*Pull,* Luther said; he proffered his hand.

Jimmy pulled Luther to a sitting position; he put his arm around Luther's shoulder to support him. Luther was already fishing for the floor with one bare foot.

Let me pull the chair up to the bed. I'll have to lay you back down for just a minute, Jimmy said.

*Pull!* (Red Queen.)

Jimmy pressed the button.

Within seconds, the nurse.

He wants to sit in the chair, Jimmy importuned.

Who turned off the air-conditioning?

I don't know, Jimmy said. (He had watched Peter turn off the air-conditioning before he left. Luther gets too cold, Peter said.)

The nurse switched the air-conditioning on. It's easier for him to breathe if the room is cool, the nurse said. To Luther: When the aides have finished what they're doing, we'll put you in the chair.

I think I can manage it, Jimmy said.

It takes three people, the nurse said; it won't be long. She raised the bed gate and covered Luther with a sheet. Luther smiled. (Harpo Marx.) The nurse left. Luther plucked the sheet away, grasped the bed gate.

*Down.*

Well, let's just wait. . . .

*Down,* said Luther. (Red Queen.) Jimmy put down the gate and sat on the edge of the bed; he put his arm around Luther's waist to prevent Luther from slipping to the floor. Luther did not acknowledge the counterforce; he grunted forward in medicated slow motion; he now had both feet on the floor.

Peter walked in.

He wants to sit in the chair, Jimmy said helplessly.

Peter snapped off the air-conditioning. He loves that chair, Peter said. All right, come on old man, Peter said. He easily transferred Luther into the recliner. Has he eaten? To Luther: Have you eaten?

Luther shook his head slowly. Smiled.

All on a summer's day.

Though I found no school in town or library or government building named in his honor, my vote for the founding father of today's Las Vegas would go to Herbert Clark Hoover, the thirty-first president of the United States. Hoover signed the bill funding the construction of the great dam that today bears his name.

In 1928 Hoover won the presidential election by a wide margin. A year later, the stock market crashed, leading to the Great Depression. Americans blamed Hoover for a financial collapse he did not cause but could not cure. Thus did Hoover, a superabundantly competent man, become a byword for incompetence. "Hoovervilles"—encampments of destitute Americans—sprang up across the country.

After President Hoover authorized the construction of the dam at Black Canyon, the state of Nevada revoked its ban on gambling. Las Vegas did not feel the brunt of the Depression, in part because as many as five thousand men found work, albeit dangerous work, building the dam. Las Vegas conspired with human nature to provide the laborers with weekend entertainments that would separate them from their pay.

In the winter of 1933, President Hoover was obliged to travel from the White House to the Capitol in the backseat of an open limousine alongside Franklin D. Roosevelt, the patrician president-elect. In a flickering news clip, we see the two men exchanging a few words as the car moves up Pennsylvania Avenue. Roosevelt spontaneously raises his hat to the crowd. Hoover's face is constrained with discomfort; he resembles W. C. Fields, the comic tragedian.

Two years later, in 1935, President Roosevelt passed through Las Vegas on his way to dedicate the new dam; he called it Boulder Dam, as did other members of his administration, and so it was called for fourteen years. Only a motion by a later Republican Congress would cement Hoover's name to the project that changed the West.

By whichever name, Hoover Dam was evidence that Nature could be harnessed: that the unruly Colorado River could be made to water the dry land of several western states, that the power generated from the controlled flow of water could light up the night.

Good Friday. Yellow tulips, closed and as thumpable as drumsticks, are massed at the entrance of the coffee shop at the Bellagio. They remind me of those phalanxes of acid-yellow flowers from behind which desert tyrants address the world with *frown, and wrinkled lip, and sneer of cold command.*

In Percy Bysshe Shelley's burlesque of royal pride, "Ozymandias," a desert traveler comes upon *two vast and trunkless legs of stone,* beside which, half buried in the sand, lies a toppled royal visage. Some long-dead artisan has incised on the monument's pedestal a deathless boast:

"My name is Ozymandias, king of kings:
Look on my works, ye Mighty, and despair!"

Over millennia, rulers of desert kingdoms, and not only rulers but prophets, and not only prophets but shepherds, but slaves, but women, have brooded on impermanence. There is not another ecology that so bewilders human vanity. Thus must palace engineers and the slaves from foreign lands be pressed into raising Pharaoh's pyramid over and against all, withstanding dynasties of sand and wind. It is a testament to the leveling humor of Las Vegas that Pharaoh's dream of eternity is mocked by the pyramid of the Luxor Hotel. The Luxor's pyramid is not made of limestone blocks but of rectangles of smoked glass that reflect and appear to change density according to the constant fluctuations of the desert sky.

In 1972 Robert Venturi, Denise Scott Brown, and Steven Izenour published an architectural monograph, *Learning from Las Vegas,* in which they celebrated the disregard for history, for propriety, for landscape in the architecture of suburban sprawl— Wienerschnitzel Chalets, Roundtable Castles, Golden Arches—an attitude best exemplified, they wrote, by the Las Vegas Strip. Their homage came at a time when East Coast architectural schools were in thrall to postwar European brutalism and city planners disregarded any necessity for delight.

In the years following the sensational Venturi–Scott Brown– Izenour essay, "old" low-rise casinos along the Strip were replaced, one by one, by grandiose hotel towers that, nevertheless, at ground level, invited tourists to inhabit cinemascopic fantasies: Rome. Egypt. Venice. Las Vegas was constructing an elaborate jest against the instinctive human fear of impermanence. Las Vegas cajoled its visitors to be amused at what the Romantic poet and the ancient prophet regard as the desert's morbid conclusion. The Eiffel Tower, the Empire State Building, Caesars Palace—

nothing in the world is rooted, nothing is permanent, nothing sacred, nothing authentic; architectural conceits are merely that.

Herbert Hoover died of a massive hemorrhage on October 20, 1964, in Suite 31-A at the Waldorf Towers in New York City. He is buried at the Herbert Hoover Library in West Branch, Iowa—the town where he was born.

No truer daughter does Las Vegas have than Dubai on the Persian Gulf, with its penthouse views of the void, its racetrack, its randy princes, its underwater hotel. Dubai and the oil-rich Arab kingdoms have purchased an architecture of mirage that is incongruous, and, therefore, defiant of the desert. Dubai has water slides, an ice palace, an archipelago of artificial islands in the shape of palm trees. The geometry that springs from the desert's plane is an assertion of human inanity in the face of natural monotony.

Even the sacred city of Mecca has taken some calibration from Las Vegas. Within the precincts of the Grand Mosque in Mecca stands the holiest site in Islam—a stone building without windows that was built in ancient days by Abraham and Ishmael. The Gate of Heaven is located directly above the cubical structure called the Kaaba. The Kaaba, covered with black silk draperies, represents the fixed point where the eternal and the temporal intersect, and around which the tide of living humanity circumambulates, counterclockwise.

For the infidel—for me—the Kaaba represents what is ancient beyond recall, but for the faithful, the Kaaba is a touchstone: affixed to a corner of the Kaaba is the Black Stone of Heaven, a stone given to Abraham by the Angel Gabriel.

Today looming over the tiny black cube is the Makkah Clock

Royal Tower, a tower reminiscent of Big Ben—a much bigger Ben—taller than the World Trade Center, with a golden crescent as its finial. Within the Makkah Clock Royal Tower is the eight-hundred-room Fairmont hotel. At its base there is a mall with four thousand shops. The Bin Laden Group, the engineering firm founded by the father of Osama bin Laden, is responsible for the overscale buildings set down upon Mecca.

Percy Bysshe Shelley died by drowning at the age of twenty-nine on July 8, 1822, when a small schooner was lost in a storm off the coast of Italy. Shelley's body was recovered from the sea and burned in a funeral pyre on the beach, after the ancient Greek fashion. Shelley's heart was not consumed by the flames and was buried under a motto devised by his friend Leigh Hunt—*Cor Cordium* ("Heart of Hearts")—in the Protestant Cemetery in Rome.

The Bellagio Conservatory and Botanical Gardens occupies a volume of cubic space reminiscent of a nineteenth-century train station. People come and go. There are hundreds of tulips and bluebells and daffodils, foxgloves, hollyhocks; there is a dense, loamy smell. There are false flora and fauna among the real—bees, ants, ladybugs, butterflies, giant poppies, toadstools. Georgic implements of gigantic scale (flowerpots, watering cans, hoes) are strewn among the flora as if abandoned by a race of giants. Most wonderful are leaping, flashing jets of water that materialize and disappear in midair. These I watch for many minutes, knowing the water or fluid must be encased in a translucent conduit, like Luther's oxygen tube, but I cannot see the tubes, cannot detect how it is done.

The Bellagio's floral exposition is a celebration of spring and does not attach itself semantically or symbolically to Easter.

On Good Friday afternoon I am stalled on Interstate 95; I am on my way to the hospice. The commuters surrounding me are headed out of town for the weekend or into town for the weekend, so there is that much of pending Easter, but nothing of Good Friday, beyond my own lonely sense of appropriate Good Friday weather (overcast, as in the Sacramento Valley of my childhood). The van ahead of me has a sign in Spanish on its bumper: ONLY GOD KNOWS IF YOU WILL RETURN. I try to recollect the Russian novel or memoir; I think it is one of the childhood reminiscences of Gorky, but the scene memory serves is too dimly lit for me to recognize the woman who stands at the window in pale, pinkish light. In fact, I do recognize her, but she is the wrong woman at the wrong window, the wrong light and season; she is a woman from a Pre-Raphaelite painting—*Mariana* by Millais—whose back is fatigued. Everything in the provincial Russian room behind the wrong woman is in readiness—the spoons, the linen, the breakfast breads, the samovar; she has stayed behind; the others have gone to midnight Mass, miles away. It is the dawn of Easter. The woman imagines the vibration of cathedral bells through the frozen air and the cracking of ice beneath the blades of the sled. Only God knows if they will return.

Luther is in bed; the head of the bed is raised. Jimmy is sitting in a chair beside the bed. Peter has gone to the airport to pick up Andrew and John. The oxygen prong is out of Luther's nose; the tube snakes under the pillow. Do you want the oxygen tube? Jimmy asks.

Luther nods.

What difference does it make? OK, something to do, I think to myself as Jimmy hooks the loop behind Luther's ears. Within two minutes Luther has torn the prong away. His breath is clotted with phlegm, like Maya Lin's *Silver River*.

Luther's eyes slide toward Jimmy on a slow tide of conscious-ness. *Light,* he says. You want the light on? Jimmy asks. *Light,* Lu-ther says again, flicking his hand slightly. Then, summoning all his power: *You are in the light.* Oh, sorry, says Jimmy; he moves his chair toward the foot of the bed. Luther flicks his hand again: *More.* Jimmy moves farther away. Luther seems momentarily de-lighted by the power of his wrist. I don't know if he means he can't see Jimmy because Jimmy is sitting in front of the window or if Jimmy is blocking light that is precious. After Jimmy makes one further move, Luther nods, smiles, sleeps. Either way.

### Entr'acte

On YouTube: The lights dim. A kettledrum rumbles through the pit as the silver limousine drives forward onto the stage's reflect-ing surface. Light pours from the proscenium like rainbow melt. The chauffeur hops to; he crosses in front of the limousine to stand at attention, his hand poised on the handle of the down-stage door. The strafing beams fuse into a single column of preter-naturally white light as the chauffeur opens the door.

Liberace emerges; Liberace unfolds; Liberace pops; his arms open wide—O glory! He wears a sequined Prince Regent suit and a white fur coat with silver lamé lining and a Queen Isabella collar as high as a wingback chair. The chauffeur kneels—knighthood is in flower—and adjusts his Master's train, twenty paces of fur car-pet. Somehow Liberace now holds a microphone (diamonds on his fingers); the chauffeur must have passed it to him when we were looking elsewhere.

Liberace questions the audience: "Do you know what kind of car this is?"

Golly.

"It is a silver Rolls-Royce. I bought it in England and brought it back here."

We bid farewell to the chauffeur. We give him a hand. His name is Thorn. Or Thor; we didn't quite . . . "We'll see more of Thor later," Liberace promises with lupine relish. Thor drives the limousine off, stage left. Another round of applause for Thor. For Rolls-Royce. For England!

Liberace addresses us as the Big Bad Wolf might address an infant or a canary or a little lamb lost—a petting voice, not un-kind. Necessarily, he supplies all the answers to his petit cate-chism. It is exactly the cadence and the Socratic method of Mister Rogers. He tugs the tonnage of his train along the lip of the stage. To some women seated in the first row: "Yes, you can feel it. Do you want to feel it? It's nice, isn't it? Do you know what it is?"

Golly.

"It is virgin fox! I had this made for a command performance I gave for Her Majesty, the Queen of England."

Press PAUSE.

Regard the rapacious eye the Wolf casts over his audience; he wets his lips as the women in the first row reach forth gingerly to pat his plush. An invitation to pull the fox's tail is an example of Las Vegas's complicated negotiation with the middle class. The middle-class tourist is invited to approach luxury on a budget, as long as she loses money. Your AARP membership card will get you an upgrade; hotcakes come with the room; parking is free. On his side of the footlights, Liberace is permitted to play the last sissy in America as long as the women in the front row agree to pretend to believe that Liberace is a great friend of the Queen of England; that Liberace is a sleeping prince who just hasn't found the right woman; that Thor has a chauffeur's license.

Liberace died on February 4, 1987, in Palm Springs, California. He is entombed in Forest Lawn Memorial Park (Hollywood Hills), Los Angeles.

The only time I hear Peter—or any of the staff at the hospice—refer to the Strip hotels, it is with reference to parking. Peter likes to park at the Flamingo; he says the exits are easy and some of the hotel's vintage modernist fixtures interest him. An aide at the hospice asks me where I am staying. "I used to park at the Bellagio," she says, "but now I park at the Renaissance." (As far as I can tell from my precious few conversations with the citizens of the real Las Vegas, the Strip is a free parking lot.)

The last time I was in Las Vegas it was to give a speech on public education. An emissary of the association I was to address picked me up at a small hotel I can't remember and drove me to a vast Greco-Gonzo extravaganza along the Strip I can't remember.

The next morning, the same emissary took me on a tour of the city before my plane departed. The Angel Moroni blew a summons eastward atop the Mormon Cathedral. Many miles of stucco; miles and miles of sky. At a café, I expressed surprise at the façade normalcy of domestic Las Vegas.

"But that's just what Las Vegas is," my companion replied. "The real Las Vegas is normal. An air force town, a university town. We are forming a symphony orchestra."

A normal American city does not have hundreds of hotels whose headliners are stitched-up gods and goddesses, whose entertainments are plumed masques, parodies of human sacrifice.

All week I have been puzzling how a city as defiant of death as Las Vegas can provide a hospice on North Buffalo Drive that is as morally and functionally serious as the one that harbors Luther.

*Solo Dios sabe si volverá.* Henry David Thoreau schoolmarmed his nineteenth-century countrymen with the assertion that one could not be a true traveler unless one left one's gate with no certainty of return. The art of walking involves an ability to saunter—the word derives from a French expression for people who have no homeland (*sans terre*), or from the French word for Holy Land—*Sainte Terre*—which became the noun used to identify religious pilgrims, *sainte-terres*. They have no particular home, Thoreau writes, but they are "equally at home everywhere."

Family trips of my childhood always began with a prayer. I suppose when one goes on vacation, one is courting death in some fashion, tying the morgue tags onto one's suitcase. But then, too, vacations are respites from death, from thoughts of death. I have sometimes wondered why friends under medical death sentences have undertaken arduous trips or undertaken arduous labors. To put some distance between themselves and death—the obvious answer.

Once, at Westminster Abbey, I paused to read the epitaph of Edmund Spencer:

> HEARE LYES (EXPECTING THE SECOND
> COMMINGE OF OVR SAVIOVR CHRIST
> IESVS) THE BODY OF EDMOND SPENCER,
> THE PRINCE OF POETS IN HIS TYME
> WHOSE DIVINE SPIRRIT NEEDS NOE
> OTHIR WITNESSE THEN THE WORKS
> WHICH HE LEFT BEHINDE HIM.
> HE WAS BORNE IN LONDON IN
> THE YEARE 1553 AND
> DIED IN THE YEARE
> 1598.

The expressed hope of dust, pronounced in a present tense, dizzied me. Westminster Abbey might crumble—must crumble—Spencer's vigil will continue until the end of time. I was leaving London that afternoon. A storm was forecast. I imagined an airplane spiraling upward into a black sky.

One can become overwhelmed on vacation—I have become so—by thinking thoughts that are too large. There is a condition identified in psychology textbooks as the Stendhal syndrome, also called, or related to, the Jerusalem syndrome, that describes a tourist's overwhelmed response to great works of art or to a sudden apprehension of scale, antiquity, multitude, death—the accompanying fear is of one's insignificance, but also of squandered opportunity.

Of course, a vacation city must be defiant of death, a desert city like Las Vegas doubly so, for it is a city built on a desolate landscape. My predicament is that I am here for death and the city of distraction is in my way.

Never had I seen blacker hair or whiter skin or a being more made for limelight. Elvis Presley appeared within a ten-thousand-watt corolla—The Messiah of Memphis. He was romantic, agile, potent. He wore a chest-baring Prince Charming jumpsuit—the "Burning Flame of Love" costume, designed by Bill Belew. Presley was already, that night in 1969, playing to the midnight sun—both feet planted in the Liberace–Peggy Lee weird. He stood very still. His nostrils dilated as though he smelled the crowd in a feral way.

I grew up in an America that shared certain narratives. It is not the same now. Everyone had seen Elvis on *The Ed Sullivan Show*; everyone had seen the photographs in the pages of *Life* magazine—photographs of Tupelo, Mississippi, where he grew up, an only child; of the haircut, when he was inducted into the army; of the sleeping private through the train window; of his parents, Vernon and Gladys—of Gladys, his mother, with such dark eyes; of his leave to visit his mother's bedside; of his mother's grave.

The platter spun at 45 rpm. The aural helix opened like a can of white-meat Apollo: an engorged voice; a slurred diction; a humpy, syrupy croon. Elvis wasn't black. He wasn't white. He wasn't masculine. He wasn't feminine. He wasn't inimitable. He was a liberator.

The theme of Elvis's show that night was the theme of Las Vegas (the gambler's prayer)—resurrection. During an interlude, between sets, the voice of a woman called through the dark in a calm voice: "Elvis, I am your mother." Immediately, several security men were weaving among the tables. Elvis did not look in the direction of the voice. He raised a bottle of Gatorade to his lips as all eyes watched the security men escort a woman in a two-piece suit through a door in the wall that closed silently behind them.

After the Elvis show, Marilyn and I went to another hotel, to a lounge that seated no more than fifty people, to watch the "Ike and Tina Turner Revue." Tina Turner whipped the Ikettes through an aggressive choreography of stiletto heels, swinging wigs; wheels of sweat spraying from the stage. The Turners were already reprising their hits from the fifties; to that extent they were furiously treading fame, sinking. (Las Vegas lounge acts are a sink.) This was two years before every Top Forty radio station in America was pumping "Proud Mary."

Elvis Presley's final performance at the Hilton Hotel was in December of 1976. He was scheduled to return the following winter. He died at Graceland, his home in Memphis, in August of 1977 at the age of forty-two. He is buried at Graceland.

Peter has gone home to change clothes. The nurse has given Luther two shots. Luther alternates between sleep (a boiling gurgle in his chest) and high-pitched, teakettle trills (bird-like, hymn-like), or he perseverates, with every exhalation, *Mama Mama Mama Mama*.

Peter returns. Luther is aware of Peter's presence; he begins to coo plaintively. I know, says Peter, I know I know I know I know. Peter massages Luther's chest. It seems to me Peter is massaging too hard, as if he would press every last drop of noxious humor from Luther's body. Luther visibly relaxes. Peter's voice, Peter's hands are the only comforts on earth.

Nomadic people of the desert have, for centuries, woven carpets that are floral meadows or geometric pleasances. Desert carpets refresh those for whom the desert is transient, repetitive. The desert is the day between the nights, the dry between the wetness of the stars. Carpets are portable gardens of repose.

At twilight, Las Vegas signs, visible from miles away, are like carpets flung up into the sky. Pulses of light chase one another about a grid of lapidary. Las Vegas signs are not so much calling the traveler to rest as calling the dead to life. Calling the loser to luck. To change. To chance.

Late in the evening we return to the hotel coffee shop and once again we pass through the Bellagio Conservatory and Botanical Gardens. Mr. McGregor's Good Earth is no longer lit from the skylight but by saturated theatrical lighting. Now I can see all the gigantic miniatures—pots and shards and all—are painted with phosphorescent colors: an installation reminiscent of Claes Oldenburg. All is hushed and holy in some trashy way, and disarmingly innocent.

All the hotels around here cast spells of one kind or another to lure you in—gondolas, snow leopards. One feels flattered. In every other city of the world, the impulse of a luxury hotel is to exclude, isolate, intimidate. Elsewhere in the world, or even a mile out of town, a looming desert or an empty sky is bent on reminding you of your insignificance—lessons of mortality, lessons of austerity, lessons of depletion. The lesson of Las Vegas is *Hey, no problemo.*

Which does not mean that Las Vegas cannot be unsettled. There was the fire of 1980 that killed eighty-five people at the MGM Grand Hotel. There was the night in October of 2003 at the theater of the Mirage Hotel: During the Siegfried and Roy show, a 380-pound tiger became distracted by someone or something in the audience. The tiger slowly turned its attention toward the auditorium and began to move downstage, unfettered. Roy Horn interposed himself between the tiger and the audience. The tiger took Horn's neck in its mouth and dragged him offstage. Some in the audience applauded.

Early in 1951, the federal government began testing atomic weapons at a site in the desert, sixty miles north of Las Vegas. At the first detonation, the roulette wheel maintained its orbit; dealers' hands did not pause. Chips rattled. Ice rattled. Customers rattled. Las Vegas resorted to its renowned humor. A bartender at one of the Strip hotels came up with an Atomic Cocktail; a beauty shop downtown advertised the Atomic Bouffant.

In 1993 Steve Wynn, at once the sultan of Las Vegas and its Tiresias (Mr. Wynn is afflicted with retinitis pigmentosa), envisioned a thirty-story luxury hotel—the world will never have seen its like—rising from the ashes of the once-fabulous Dunes.

On a calm October evening, therefore, two hundred thousand spectators lined Las Vegas Boulevard South. Heralded by cannonade from the pirate ship harbored in the lagoon of the Treasure Island Hotel (another of Wynn's visions), the south wing of the Dunes Hotel—not yet forty years old—was dynamite-imploded. The crowds cheered.

Back in the sixties, when the "old" Dunes was running at full-tilt, a thirty-five-foot fiberglass sculpture of a raffish sultan stood over the entrance to the hotel, as upon a parapet, to welcome travelers to his desert kingdom. Tastes change. The kitsch idol was eventually removed to the hotel's golf course as a relict of the age of personified brands. One day an electrical short in some chamber of the sultan's heart caused him to melt to the ground. The city of antique lands was amused by the tragic kismet.

Luther and Peter moved to Las Vegas because their apartment building in Berkeley was converting to condominiums. For what it would cost to buy their two-bedroom apartment, they could get a new house in Las Vegas. Peter was enthusiastic; Luther was iffy, but if that was what Peter wanted.

Initially, we heard excitement about their house. Luther's medications, though, were not controlling his condition as effectively as they once had. He was tired all the time; there was nowhere to walk; you had to get in the car and drive to a mall if you wanted to take a walk. Luther couldn't drive because he couldn't see; he had various cancers—of the eye, of the jaw. Whenever Jimmy called, Luther was just watching TV, watching Miss Oprah.

But then Luther found a new doctor, someone efficacious. New meds! Turns out, the drugs should have been changed years ago. Luther began to feel well and he began to feel better about Las Vegas. He liked the extremes of it—the heat, the cold, the flats, the mountains. He liked being a house owner in the desert—the strangeness of it! He said he felt like a pioneer. He talked about special window treatments, solar screens—unknown in Northern California. Barack Obama ran for president and Luther's HIV was undetectable.

Now that Luther lies dying three miles away, we finally visit his house. I am in the backyard with Peter. Peter has observed that some neighbors persist in planting grass. The summer burns it all away. Come September, the lawns need to be reseeded. When Peter and Luther wanted to plant some trees, they had to call out a contractor with machines of the sort that are used in mines. Look, Peter says, attempting to dig with his heel in the backyard dirt. The desert refuses his heel.

I ask Peter if he and Luther ever go down to the Strip to see the shows. Only when friends come to town, he says. People in town rarely go. Though there are special rates for townies. The musicians that interest Luther—singles and groups from the sixties—often play the lounges at smaller hotels, and they sometimes go to those.

The Moulin Rouge hotel and casino opened on the west side of town in 1955 and catered to a black clientele. Nat King Cole, Louis Armstrong, Lena Horne, Pearl Bailey, and many other stars performed there. The Original Sin of Sin City had nothing to do with the sexual gaming Las Vegas now advertises. Las Vegas—the western town, the Mormon town, the mobster town, the stardust town—was a Jim Crow town well into the 1960s. Las Vegas granted dispensations to excess only within limits—white limits.

Black entertainers could perform at the Strip casinos, but they could not eat or drink or gamble or take rooms in them. This story may be as apocryphal as the rest of Las Vegas: One evening, exiting the stage door of a famous hotel and crossing the pool area, Dorothy Dandridge slipped off one of her pumps to cool her foot in the pool. Someone observed Miss Dandridge—an employee or a guest. The management of the hotel had the pool drained and scoured.

Holy Saturday afternoon. Luther seemed more heavily sedated than on Friday. The bed was level; the air-conditioner was off.

A young man's head appeared from around the door. Glasses. Balding. Do you know . . . ? His entire body slid into the room, leaving the door as it was. Does Mister . . . Do you know if Mr. Thomas has any religious affiliation?

Baptist, said Jimmy, standing up. Raised Baptist; he went to several churches along the way, but.

I'm not a Baptist minister, said the young man. In fact, I'm not a minister; I'm studying to become a chaplain. Don Jensen. Hi. Do you think Mr. Thomas would object to a prayer?

No, I'm sure not, said Jimmy. (Later, when recounting the chaplain's visit to Peter, Jimmy learned that Luther had been confirmed as a Lutheran in Berkeley.)

Mr. Jensen had sweat rings under his arms. Jimmy indicated Mr. Jensen should take the chair near the bed. Mr. Jensen leaned forward to speak directly into Luther's ear. Mr. Jensen did not raise his voice. Luther did not stir.

Honestly, you never know who will attend your last hours. When my friend Marty's mother was dying, they called the rectory for a priest. There was no priest available. Really? No priest? Not a one, said a woman at the answering service. The hospice had a rabbi on call. How about a rabbi? In the end, Marty's mother liked the rabbi so well she canceled her order for a priest.

You are a lucky man, Mr. Thomas. Mr. Jensen spoke calmly into Luther's ear. It is a great blessing to die on Easter Sunday. Our Lord rose from the dead and tore off his shroud and tossed it in a corner like so much dirty laundry. Then he walked out into the first light of sunrise and the gates of his kingdom were opened forevermore. You will enter into that kingdom this very day. Jimmy looked to the palm tree in the parking lot, then back to the face of the man speaking calmly into Luther's ear. If there is anything that is holding you back, any misgiving, let us resolve it now in the love of God. Believe God loves you, Mr. Thomas. I am going to say the words our Savior taught us. You follow along as best you can: Our Father, Who art in heaven, hallowed be Thy name. Thy kingdom come, Thy will be done, on earth as it is in heaven. Give us this day our daily bread and forgive us our trespasses as we forgive those who trespass against us, and lead us not into temptation but deliver us from evil. For thine is the kingdom and the power and the glory for ever and ever. Amen.

Mr. Jensen stood; he traced a cross upon Luther's forehead with his thumb; he nodded to Jimmy; he left the room.

If he couldn't make it home for Easter, Luther would always send his mother a check so she could buy herself a new Easter outfit, a dress and a hat—a great big old Pizarro hat, as he called the wide brims and short crowns she favored.

One day, when Luther was four or five, he looked up and saw a tiny silver plane crossing the sky. *Look, Mama,* he said. His mother was pinning clothes on the line. *When I grow up I am going to ride through the sky like that.* His mother looked up where he pointed, then bent once more to her basket. *Mama, you're sad because you think I never will, but I will.*

"Class," Bugsy Siegel remarked, "that's the only thing that counts in life. Class. Without class and style a man's a bum; he might as well be dead."

Holy Saturday. It is the last hour of Sabbath for the Jews—the setting of the sun. Cher's face, bedizened with jewels, floats over the Strip like a Byzantine icon. A large crowd of pedestrians makes an aimless *paseo* among the hotels.

I am making my way up Las Vegas Boulevard to the Easter Vigil Mass at Guardian Angel Cathedral, just beyond the Wynn. At intersections, escalators transport pedestrians to crossways over the streets. Along both sides of the overpass corridor are Mexican families selling bottled water from ice chests. The prices are better than in the hotel shops and people do buy. There are long lines of touts—young Mexican men who snap advertisement cards together, as one might oppose two playing cards to make a clicking sound like the stops on a wheel of fortune. I accept a few cards to see what they are. One is for a bar called the Library. The others entitle the bearer to a dollar off a drink or a ten percent discount or some similar enticement to seek out one among the hundreds of lounges and casinos in the hotels along the Strip and downtown.

To get to the overpass, the pedestrian must thread his way through a cul-de-sac of shops—like Paris, I hear one tourist say; like Jerusalem, I think to myself. There is no other way to cross the street. The crowd is aimless, the crowd is distracted, the crowd is expectant, the crowd feels lucky. The Strip is actually rigidly controlled. Taxis cannot pick up or leave off passengers on the street, but only at hotels. There are entertainments that are free— the dancing waters, the pirate ship, the Roman gods with animated eyes—but these are hotel inducements. I don't notice any buskers on the streets; they would interfere with the flow; the flow is everything; a great deal of money depends on the flow.

I had taken a walk earlier Saturday morning to locate the cathedral and to learn the hour of the Easter Vigil Mass. I passed the pirate ship on my way and I studied it for a time. The crow's nest was shrouded in drab velvet—obviously the stage for some eventual derring-do. Riggings and ladders would be climbed; the mast would be descended. The pirate ship looked down at heel as, I suppose, a pirate ship ought. At that hour of a Saturday morning, the pirates were still in their beds, somewhere in the real Las Vegas.

But now I pass the ship in twilight. The velvet curtain is thrown open (and as red as one could wish it under theatrical lighting). The pirate captain brandishes his sword (white-hot as a laser) to signal the cannonade; the ship is enveloped in fogs of colored smoke. (Tolstoy's description of the Battle of Borodino: colored smokes, fairyland.)

One's purpose is buffeted by the confusion of entertainments and architectures. There are loudspeakers in every palisade, under every hedge, overhead in every arcade. Huge digital screens on the sides of hotels project *David Copperfield Live!* One's thoughts are not one's own. This is some other syndrome. The Happy Hour syndrome. The Happiest Place on Earth syndrome. This must be how non-Christians feel at Christmastime (the Jewish antiquaire, played by Erland Josephson, making his way through the darkening streets of Stockholm in Ingmar Bergman's *Fanny and Alexander*).

By the time I pass the Wynn, the crowds thin and the Strip recedes. I see a Thai restaurant and the cathedral behind it. The main doors of the church are locked. I am late. I enter through a side door. The place is packed; an usher directs me into the choir loft where there are some families with children but the majority are solitary latecomers like me. I take a pew behind a woman whose posture I read as burdened.

The Cathedral of the Guardian Angel belongs to the modest Las Vegas of the fifties and sixties—of low-rise hotels and casinos. Moe Dalitz, a reputed mobster in Cleveland and a revered philanthropist in Las Vegas, donated the land for the construction of the church and selected the architect, Paul R. Williams, an African American, who had designed Frank Sinatra's house and other celebrity homes in Palm Springs. Two marble angels flank the altar—the sort of angels one might see in any nineteenth-century cemetery. Behind the altar is a large mosaic mural of the softest modernist declension—intersecting mandala (free form rather than cubist), and within the mandala are several emergent figures; foremost is Jesus. The figures free themselves of shroud-like encumbrances. It is Resurrection as the Ballet Russe de Monte Carlo or the Ice Follies might conceive of Resurrection. The mural is poor religious art but it is profoundly in period—a period after World War II; a spirit of resurrection exemplified by Coventry Cathedral, the United Nations, the founding of Israel, the Salk vaccine, the Second Vatican Council. As its period coincides with the period of my poor soul's formation, I am forgiving of the mural's ecstatic silliness, its inchoate hope.

In the balcony of the cathedral, I find myself aligned with banks of loudspeakers suspended stage left of the nave.

The Epistle is performed theatrically. A man wearing a gray turtleneck rises from the congregation—he is miked; he is Saint Paul—to address us intimately, urgently, from the first century. In fact, I have always wanted to see this done, and it is done very well. But it does not please me for being so thoroughly done. There is no pleasing me tonight.

The bishop sits on his throne like Old King Cole, his head resting on his hand. The Mass proceeds as a series of divertissements, in the manner of the Royal Ballet—attempts to rouse the bishop from his unaccountable melancholy. The master of ceremonies tries everything—baptisms, confirmations, fiddlers three. Nothing seems to work.

Peter returned to the hospice with Andrew and John. Luther seemed to know his friends were there. He struggled to open his eyes and he finally succeeded, his eyes sliding beneath their sliced lids. Did he see? Yes, we thought he did.

Then the nurse came in and she said they were going to bathe Luther and make him more comfortable. She asked us to wait outside. While we waited in the corridor, three women—the nurse and two aides—filed past us with armfuls of folded sheets and towels.

The three women were not solemn. We heard their light, cheerful voices through the door, as if they were dressing a bride. Then we heard a heart-rending aw-w-w-w—the sound women make when an infant does something adorable. Did Luther say something? Or make a gesture of some kind? Then we heard an outburst of laughter that as quickly became consolation: Oh, honey, it's alright, it's alright. (Was Luther weeping?)

By and by, the door opened; the women left, their eyes downcast. We filed back into the room. They had turned Luther three-quarters on his side. He was leaning upon a bank of several pillows, as Christ leans upon a rock in paintings of Gethsemane. They had arranged him for his Passion. He was gasping. His teeth were bared. My heart involuntarily pronounced aw-w-w aw-w-w-w aw-w-w-w.

After a scintillating "Alleluia"—the loudspeakers buzzing with cymbal sizzle—all in the congregation stand as the Easter Gospel is proclaimed in the cathedral. When the Sabbath was over, Mary of Magdala, Mary the mother of James, and Salome, bought spices with which to go and anoint him. And very early in the morning on the first day of the week they went to the tomb when the sun had risen.

It was called the Dogwood tree.

I leave immediately after Communion. Outside, a black desert wind. (The forecast for Easter morning is for showers and dust storms. Aren't those antithetical?) Though he risks a fine for doing so, a cabbie—Pakistani or Indian—picks me up on the sidewalk along Las Vegas Boulevard South. Business has been lousy, he shrugs; he took a chance. He asks why I am in town. I tell him about Luther. He tells me about a cousin of his who is dying of cancer.

All along the bright holiday boulevard, he describes a woman dying alone on the other side of the world, under tomorrow's sun. He drops me off on the shore of Lago di Como, on the Eiffel Tower side.

Luther Thomas died Easter Sunday, April 4, 2010.

# four

# Tour de France

A knucklehead fell out of a tree.

The judge had promised us, the twelve of us, a trial lasting no more than two days. It was not until the fifth day that the plaintiff (a flat-voiced teenaged boy) took the stand to explain why he had climbed a tree in Golden Gate Park in the first place, how he ended up on the ground with a broken arm.

*Just foolin' around.*

The boy's parents' lawyer claimed the park maintenance crew of the city and county of San Francisco should have cut the dead wood out of the tree.

Personal injury. The phrase summons scars more recently sustained, and another summer, when I was lying on a bed in St. Mary's hospital in San Francisco, thinking about Aix-en-Provence.

My thorax had been unpacked and repacked like one of those fire-hose boxes you see in old buildings. A foot or so of O-gauge track burned down my belly whenever I raised myself, whenever I twisted to answer the phone.

On a television set hanging from the ceiling, Lance Armstrong, cancer survivor extraordinaire, was making a triumphal progress up the lime-leafed Champs-Élysées. I forget which among his victories this was.

Whatever else cancer is, cancer is a story that leads away from home. Even the luckiest stories involve harrowing prompts and trials. Lance Armstrong endured trials so dire I have seen him weep in the recounting of them on TV.

My cancer story began in Paris, also on a bed, where I was watching the aftermath of the Madrid train bombings on television. I had been troubled for several weeks by night sweats. I was due to travel to Spain in two days. The doctors were not initially concerned. Some low-grade infection, perhaps to do with prostate.

No doctor I consulted subsequently ever uttered the word "cancer." The oncologist told me the X-rays showed a growth two inches long. "Growth" is a word I had previously associated with maturation, even wisdom. The unaccountable burst of inches after a childhood summer. Or the daffodils in Hyde Park after that first lonely winter of graduate school. The oncologist's growth was some kind of ghostly scallop, a story-eater.

My first impulse was responsible and mundane. Update my will. Get my tax returns in order. Ask a thoroughly unsentimental friend to serve as my medical executor.

My next impulse was to visit a Dominican priest. At this juncture, I entered a second euphemism.

I am a Roman Catholic old enough to have grown up calling the seventh sacrament of the church *Extreme Unction*. There was no mistaking a sacrament with such a name. One summoned a priest to the bedside of a relative to anoint the care-worn forehead with holy oil. The ceremony was so wedded to death in the Catholic imagination that the concern of irresolute relatives was always that poor old Nonno would wake up to see a priest fussing about him and die of fright.

So as not to frighten Nonno, therefore, the Catholic Church

has jettisoned the term and now refers to the "Anointing of the Sick."

That is what I got. I got oil on my forehead and hands. And then I asked the Dominican priest, who is a friend of mine, to hear my confession.

I had not been to confession for several decades—a sin in itself. You might imagine I left many trash bags full of sins in the priest's office that afternoon.

*Bless me father, for I have sinned. This is my first confession in thirty-two years. . . .*

The substance of my confession is the conclusion of the story. I will return to the parish rectory and what I discovered in preparing to confess three decades of my life. But, first, I need to explain why it was that, even as Lance Armstrong rode, like ancient Paris, past cheering crowds, I was thinking about Aix-en-Provence while recuperating at St. Mary's.

I have never been to Aix-en-Provence. My best friend in college, Ted Mayhew—of course, that is not Ted's real name—had passed a defining summer there. I was forever pestering Ted about places in the world he had seen and I had not. My curiosity on the subject of Aix elicited from Ted only disparagement of his parents, particularly his mother, with whom he was perpetually annoyed.

When he was sixteen years old, Ted stayed two months with friends of his parents in Aix. He spent that summer drawing and painting. Ted's ambition was to be an artist. I hadn't known that. He returned home to New York with three water-plumped sketchbooks. He put the sketchbooks away on a shelf in his bedroom before he returned to his New England prep school in September.

In November, when he came home for Thanksgiving, Ted noticed his sketchbooks were out on the dining room table. He took them back to his room.

On the Friday after Thanksgiving, his mother summoned Ted to the living room for a grown-up chat. She had taken the liberty of showing Ted's sketchbooks and watercolors to an elderly and well-known society painter. The old man had looked over Ted's work and opined the boy would not amount to more than an amateur. His talent was not large enough.

Ted's mother had several voices. When she portrayed pragmatism, she had recourse to New England. It was his mother's bad Katharine Hepburn that killed Ted: *Knot. Lodge. Nuff.*

Ted never picked up a paintbrush again.

In the years since that summer morning at St. Mary's hospital, I have sat among bald women in doctors' offices. We all read— and reread by mistake—the well-worn issues of *People* magazine. Thus have I attended the idylls of Brad and Angelina and all the remote bright stars.

From those same issues of *People* magazine I have come to learn the sequence of women in Lance Armstrong's life—from wife Kristin to Sheryl Crow to someone named Tory, and a much younger Ashley. Most recently, there was an "amicable separation" from Kate Hudson.

I seem to remember it was Sheryl Crow who was waiting for Lance Armstrong on that summer day in Paris. He wore the yellow jersey that represented laurel.

One day, while visiting the Mayhews' Manhattan apartment, I admired Ted's watercolor of a rose-covered wall in Aix-en-Provence. His mother had given it a prominent place in the room, surely denoting some pride, I ventured. *Only because it matches her peach-colored walls,* Ted replied in Brunswick blue.

The Filipina nursing assistant (half my age, with sorrowing eyes) stood beside my bed, adeptly silencing the alarm of the drip monitor.

*Beautiful flowers,* she said. She meant on the windowsill.

Take them, I said.

*Really, you don't want them?*

I want you to have them, I said. Left unsaid: On so many mornings, dear Filipina-stranger-checking-my-vitals, you have bathed my torso and legs and back. You have brought what clutter and cheer you could to this sterile room. You deserve the flowers on the windowsill, for you are like spring.

Though what I have learned from being around the sick and the dying is that it is one thing to clean a stranger, quite another thing to wipe your father or your mother. Intimacy changes everything.

I would extend this generalization to cover the matter of personal injury. It is one thing to suffer hurt from a tree in Golden Gate Park, but quite another to suffer an injury from a parent, a lover, a best friend, a teacher whose favorite you thought yourself to be.

Strangers drop hydrogen bombs on strangers. But when you were in fourth grade, your best friend blabbed your secret to a cafeteria table of boys. Your best friend did this only to get a laugh.

Though it was Sunday my oncologist came into the hospital room just as Lance Armstrong ascended the dais. The oncologist was leaving the next day on vacation. A doctor with a Polish surname would take over on Monday.

The oncologist pulled back the sheet. Over his shoulder, Lance Armstrong kissed the several hired Graces whose fate it was to bestow his prize. The doctor unbuttoned my hospital tunic. The crowd cheered. "Healing nicely," he said, admiring the gathering of my flesh. I did not look.

Will it go away? The scar, I meant.

"Nope, sorry," the doctor said. "But it is my impression that women like men with scars."

Bulls like men with scars. Mine reminds me of Andy Warhol's scar after a madwoman shot him in the stomach. Even that is to beg some heroic cast. My scar looks like the seam up the front of a Teddy Bear.

*Bless me, father, for I have sinned.*

After three unshriven decades, what I discovered, in rehearsing my failures as a human being, was not how many sins I had committed, but how small they were.

*Bless me, father, I have lived my life in lowercase.*

No Joycean blasphemy. No Miltonic grandeur. Only so many homely cruelties, inflicted without much thought or care.

To summarize: I was the boy in fourth grade who told my best friend's secret, to get a laugh. I do not even remember what the secret was.

Do you suppose he does? Even small wounds have long consequences. After three unshriven decades, what frightened me most during my *examen* was the realization that I had nurtured so many small wounds inflicted on *me*.

That was what I was thinking about as cancer survivor extraordinaire, Mr. Lance Armstrong, coasted up the Avenue des Champs-Élysées. The boy crashing out of the tree like a lumpen sloth. My best friend in fourth grade scalded by laughter. The sensible Park Avenue matron killing her artistic son as blithely as she would twist a bright bow.

Sheryl Crow bit her lip, turned away as though the sun were in her eyes. Brilliant Lance Armstrong raised thin arms over his head in triumph.

I seem to remember it was Sheryl Crow who was waiting that summer day. Perhaps I misremember. Perhaps it was Tory. Or Helen of Troy.

# five

# Darling

## 1. Theatricals

You never met Helen, did you? My younger sister. Helen and I used to pretend. I was Murray Perahia and she was the Duchess of Alba, stepping up to the maître d', beads of sweat dripping from our credit cards onto the carpets of London, of Paris. People did turn. I was Al Pacino and she was the Duchess of Zuiderzee-sur-Mer and Swansdown. We avoided their stares. I was that Indian tennis star—I've forgotten his name. We requested a table in a quiet corner. Helen sold off her duchy; she was Tina Chow or somebody like that; Marguerite Gautier. She was the Countess de Gooch ("Fabulous wealth, the de Gooches!"). Helen spent her youth memorizing *Auntie Mame* and the Marx Brothers. ("Is my aunt Minnie in here?") Our desperate drollery snagged on table linens, waggled the ice buckets as we were forward-marched to our table. Not a bad table, either, considering.

I was the lonely gay brother with a fellowship abroad who lived in a bed-sit in Chelsea; who kept a stack of coins on the mantel to feed into a slot in the gas heater; who brought Indian take-out back to my room on Sundays; who read John Milton and *Harpers & Queen* beneath the lowest cone of a tricolor pole lamp (turquoise, chartreuse, orange) that blinked whenever Mr. Okeke charged across my ceiling.

Helen was my hardheaded disciple, my treasurer, my Galatea.

Now that she was grown and had a job working for a bank in California, she thought she might as well drop by London for Easter, pokey little London, she said, whereas the flowers were already out in Paris.

Darling, I would say, as waiters circled us in magic, will you have a sweet? No inflection was too outlandish for Helen; no serve went unreturned: "Why do we leave brown coffee-burble stains on our cups and nobody else does?" Tina Chow looked bemusedly across the dining room; she studied the chaste coffee cups she saw other diners lower from their lips. "I'll have the Indian pudding, please."

"Darling" is a voluble endearment exchanged between lovers on stage and screen. The noun is overblown, dirigible; strikes the American ear as insincere. Nevertheless, "darling" became a staple of married life on American television in the fifties: Good morning, darling. Remember, darling, the Bradshaws are coming for dinner tonight. What's wrong, darling?

"Darling" was a most common salutation in letters between soldiers and their wives or girlfriends during World War II. Lovers surprised themselves in the act of portraying themselves with a heightened diction—in that way attempting to convey an awareness that their lives were drawn by Tolstoyan engines of history.

One night in Boston I went out to dinner with my editor and his wife—this was my first editor, the beloved editor, and I was in awe of him; I still am in awe of him. The editor kissed me on the cheek as we parted and called me his "darling boy," as if thereby investing me with the Order of Letters Genteel. It was among the happiest nights of my life; I was filled with sadness as I watched the two of them, the editor and his wife, walk away.

In Neo-classical and Romantic poetry, "darling" is an adjective bestowed upon innocence: darling curls, darling buds. Darling boys.

In stage-Irish, "darling" is ironic, yet still a sentiment bestowed: Sure and you're a darling man altogether, Jack Boyle!

But then the post-lapsarian actress Tallulah Bankhead blared "darling" like a foghorn—fair warning to anyone of sincerity or true affection. By democratizing the endearment, by addressing everyone as "darling"—intimate or stranger, friend or foe—she produced a brilliant comic effect.

You never met Nell, did you? No, you wouldn't have. Nell never liked L.A. Back then, when Nell and I were Beatrice and Benedick of the graduate division, we were more than a bit much. We were alert to the slightest vibration of irony in one another, of pointed glance or quiver of lip or inflection—those stiff twin compasses had nothing on us. Nell! And she looked the very Hogarth of a Nell, a wine-red laugh and green eyes, curly hair and rollicking shoes—any "darling" I sent Nell's way was a struck match to an arsenal of pent theatricality: tosses of mane, wreaths of smoke, crossings of leg. At a bacon-and-eggs café on Telegraph Avenue we favored with our presence, we carried on like the Lunts.

"Look, darling, someone's drunk up all my wine."

Have some of mine.

"But yours is gone, too."

And we can't afford any more.

"Sad. And the sun's gone down."

And the Master's not home.

Just so was "darling" a prop for Cary Grant—as careless a conveyance of cooled emotion as a cigarette case or a fountain pen—an advertisement of his acquaintanceship with ease, ease with life, ease with women, whether he was playing the thief or the playboy

or the soldier. The Cary Grant performance was in homage to another lower-middle-class Englishman, Nöel Coward. Growing up
in Teddington, Coward imagined a leisured class of world-weary
sophisticates whose conversations were rank with "darlings."
"Darlings" didn't mean anything. "Darlings" were objective-
nominative vagaries, starlings in a summer sky. "Darlings" were
sequined grace notes flying by at the famous Coward clip—Coward
designed his lines to be spoken rapidly and unemphatically.

Something about this personal-classical, asexual, theatrical
form of address interested me, pleased me. I studied how to use it.

### 2. The Garden of Eden

Helen and Nell saw the fun of it immediately. You, on the other
hand, were my first unwilling darling. L.A. is a city so full of darlings, I couldn't understand your resistance at first.

The day your divorce was finalized, we drove up the coast to
the Garden of Eden. A right turn off the Coast Highway at the
bait-and-tackle shop and halfway up a hill. No view at all. The air
was fresh. There was nothing camp about the Garden of Eden but
the sign—a neon palm tree bedizened with a hot pink snake. It
was a hotel with cabins from the thirties that had been refur-
bished to sea drift–moderne. The building was badly damaged by
a mudslide in the nineties and is no more. But on a weekday afternoon, in 1982, it was the perfect respite from L.A.

On second thought, Darling, I said, surveying the restaurant
through the side window, let's not eat in the dining room; let's go
through to the bar and order club sandwiches.

*Fine.*

Fine as volcanic ash is fine? Fine as an anvil dropped from the
Empire State Building is fine? We were great chums a moment
ago. What's up? You prefer the dining room?

*The bar is fine . . .* DARLING.

Broken yolk. Call 911. I steered you, as I would have steered a fizzing depth charger, through the placid mirrors of the Garden of Eden, into the bar. Two clubs, please. They made them with chopped olives, remember? Two clubs and one beer. And one coffee. Black. Black as pork blood. Black as shark bile. Black as . . .

*I will have the Syrah, please.*

Sorry. One beer, one Syrah. Skip the coffee.

Ex was on your mind, I knew that. You were on edge. I was never the Other Man, careful on that score. I made you laugh, though. Ex was grateful. OK, it was "darling" that pissed you off.

One redhead. Chin resting on hand. The snake's neon tongue flicked long, short, long, short.

One pretender.

### 3. Habeebee

"Darling," Andrew says, with a good-humored sigh. He writes the Arabic word on his napkin with a fountain pen; the ink bleeds away from the word.

"Come weez me to zee casbah," American children learned to say from cartoons without the least idea what a casbah might be. Some kind of nightclub, I imagined, for Shriners. In the course of writing this chapter, I ask Andrew who lives in Cairo to explain to me—not a parlor game, not quite; I am truly interested—how it is possible, in what way is it possible, I mean, for an Arab to address a man, another man, affectionately, as "darling." Still imagining the casbah.

The feminine noun, pronounced *habib-tea,* might be spoken to a wife, to a family member, to a child, to Mata Hari, to Hedy Lamarr.

The masculine noun is pronounced *habeebee.* While it is not advisable to address one's employer or a policeman with such a noun, my friend instructs, one might, in a playful manner—with irony, I assume—address a waiter or a cab driver as "darling." You might be surprised, too, he says, when a man you met for the first time only a few hours earlier phones you at your hotel and opens with a Tallulah, as in: *Habeebee*, why have I not heard from you?

The admirable intimacy and the demonstrative physicality of Arab men among themselves seem to depend on the separation of men from women before marriage, and a curatorial regard of women after marriage, and the consequent mystery and the consequent male anxiety about women—their scarves and blooded rags and watchful eyes—from birth to death. In a region of mind without coed irony, where women are draped like Ash Wednesday statues (as too hot to handle) and stoned to death on an accusation of adultery (as too insignificant to cry over), men, among themselves, have achieved an elegant ease of confraternity and sentimentality.

Do you remember, Darling, we were sitting in the ICU waiting room at UCLA Medical Center when two Arab men, thirties, handsome—one the father, one the uncle, we supposed—entered with two children, two boys? The boys played; the men talked. A tall woman wearing a black veil entered. Her face was exposed. Her complexion was ashen; there were dark circles under her eyes; she was preoccupied, talking into a cell phone. Her burning eyes strafed the room. The men leaned away from each other, stopped talking. The children got up from the floor and took seats. She briefly spoke to the men then left the room, still talking into the cell phone.

The children returned to the floor. The men recommenced their conversation; they spoke Arabic to each other but English to the children. By and by, one of the men, the uncle, lifted one of the boys to his knee. "So, my darling," he said, "do you want to go to Mecca with them? Or will you come to Medina with me?" At which he kissed the boy's forehead so juicily that we immediately turned to each other to mouth: Medina!

A teacher invited me to my niece's prep school classroom to give a talk, and I entered the classroom at 9:05 a.m., how-do-you-do, etcetera. There was my niece in the first row. "Hello, darling"—I addressed her in the familial vernacular in front of ALL her friends. My sister reported to me later that my niece had wanted to DIE. At fifteen, I guess she was a year or two shy of being able to relish a gay uncle in public.

She didn't die. She grew up to be an absolute darling. And a player.

When I was fifteen, I attended a Catholic boys' high school. I prospered well enough. In an all-boys school, as in a patriarchal theocracy, sexual roles are distributed widely. The absent feminine must still be accounted for, as in an all-boys' production of *Julius Caesar*. Roles of pathos were available to boys at my high school, but I eschewed them in favor of a role more akin to Prosecutor, Ironist. I advanced by questions. In some more perfect world, like *American Bandstand*, I suppose I would have been happier in a sexually integrated high school. I knew how to talk to girls. I had two sisters. And I loved to talk. But early nonsexual female companionship would have come at a price. "Sissy" is the chrysalis of "darling."

As a boy, I resisted the aunts' encouragement to go outside with my cousins or to join the group of men standing around the gaping hood of a car, silently regarding an exposed horsepower. I preferred to linger with the women, to listen to gossip, to hear irony concerning the projects of men—irony I was fully capable of sharing.

During my high school years, a boy from my neighborhood named Malcolm chose me to be his friend for a season. His elbow nudged my book in the public library one Saturday afternoon as he sprawled forward across the table feigning some condition— boredom, I suppose. His voice was like shadow—as whispery and as indistinct as shadow, due to an adolescent change. "Do you want to wrestle?" he asked.

I have never met anyone since who speaks as Malcolm spoke: He daydreamed; he pronounced strategies out loud (as I raked elm leaves from our lawn and piled them in the curb)—about how he would befriend this boy or that boy, never anyone I knew; Malcolm went to a different high school. "First," he said, "I will tease him about his freckles. Then I will tease him about his laugh—how his laugh sounds a little like a whinny sometimes. I won't go too far. You should see how his wrist pivots as he dribbles down the court.

"He's got these little curls above his sideburns. I wish I had those." (He would catch me up on the way to the library.) "What are you reading? We read that last year. Not really a war story, though, is it? Want to go eat French toast?"

Malcolm had a car and an after-school grocery-delivery route and a criminal penchant. I knew, because he told me, he'd been caught breaking into empty houses.

He walked like an illustration from *Huckleberry Finn*—arms akimbo, fingers spread, picking up his knees as though he were stepping over creaking floorboards. He had dark eyes, very white skin, and an expression of condescending pity like that of a raptor bird, if raptor birds had eyes that dark. He said he was part Chickasaw.

What is a season in the life of a high school boy? Four months or so. Malcolm's next season was girls. Basketball and girls.

On summer nights, my mother and Helen and I stayed up late watching old movies. At some point in the movie the women would retire from the table and leave the men to their brandy and cigars. I preferred movies that followed the women upstairs to a region of knowing. . . .

The doorbell rang at eleven thirty.

My mother went to the upstairs front window. I went down to answer the bell. It was Malcolm.

"Come out for a minute," Malcolm whispered.

I closed the door behind me.

"Smell this," he said, thrusting his index finger under my nose. I did not understand.

He named a girl I did not know. He was ecstatic. He leaned backward on his legs and silently crowed. He jumped from the top porch step down to the sidewalk. He ran away, down the street. I never heard that audacious male voice again. Unfleshed echoes in *Les Liaisons dangereuses,* perhaps, or the memoirs of Casanova, but never again the naked envy of the seducer.

### 4. *Picasso*

Because I had arrived early for my nephew's wedding in Golden Gate Park, I decided to walk over to the de Young Museum to look at an exhibition from the Musée Picasso in Paris. Many of the paintings displayed Picasso's naked infatuation with female-ism, with convexity, concavity, bifurcation. The female face, too, was divided into competing arrondissements—one tearful, one tyrannical—like the faces of playing-card Queens.

Concurrent with the Picasso there was an exhibit at the museum of the fashion of Cristóbal Balenciaga, another Spaniard, Picasso's contemporary. But whereas the sexed, sublime painter undressed women as unashamedly as if he had created them, the modernist couturier made formidable casings for women, unassailable pods, chitins, scapulars, shields—made saints of women, made queens, bullfighters, pagodas, nurses, priests, Jeannes d'Arc—conventuals of the Order of Fashion who, thus armed, might one day slay the grizzled minotaur of the maze-like gallery upstairs.

I was the one who insisted it was time for you to lose the jeans and the sweatshirts, Darling. I sat through a rainy Saturday afternoon on a fake Louis Quinze chair in a salon at the Beverly Hills I. Magnin as the Delphic vendeuse consulted her clattering racks to bring forward a succession of looks for you to try. Patience, Darling, I cautioned—I could tell you were about to bolt. The stockroom door opened one more time, and the priestess stepped forward, bearing in her arms a red Chanel cocktail dress that betokened revenge on a shallow, faithless husband.

A middle-aged woman in a brown wool suit tapped my shoulder after Mass. She knew my name. She said she had read an interview I gave to an online magazine on the gay marriage controversy in California. At that time, a Catholic archbishop colluded with officials from the Church of Jesus Christ of Latter-day Saints in a campaign to protect the sacred institution of marriage from any enlarging definition (including civil marriage, which the Catholic Church does not recognize as sacramentally valid). Campaign checks to be made payable to the Knights of Columbus.

The Knights of Columbus is a lay fraternal organization sanctioned by the Catholic Church. The Knights are an admirable bunch of guys—I believe "guys" is the right word—who spend many hours performing works of charity. On festival days, the Knights get themselves up with capes and swords and plumed hats like a comic-opera militia.

The woman in the brown suit did not say she agreed with my comments in the article; she did not say she disagreed. She said: "I am a Dominican nun; some days I cannot remember why."

I will stay in the Church as long as you do, I said.

Chummy though my reply was, it represented my abrogation of responsibility to both the Church and the nun.

A gay man easily sees himself as expendable in the eyes of the Church hierarchy because that is how he imagines the Church hierarchy sees him. The Church cannot afford to expel women. Women are obviously central to the large procreative scheme of the Church. Women have sustained the Church for centuries by their faith and their birthrates. Following the sexual scandals involving priests and children, women may or may not consent to present a new generation of babies for baptism. Somewhere in its canny old mind, the Church knows this. Every bishop has a mother.

It is because the Church needs women that I depend upon women to protect the Church from its impulse to cleanse itself of me.

I shook hands with the Dominican nun and we parted.

But even as I type these words, the Vatican has initiated a campaign against American nuns who (according to the Congregation for the Doctrine for the Faith) promote "radical feminist themes" and who remain silent regarding their Excellencies' positions on women's reproductive rights and homosexuality. A nun's silence is interpreted as dissent in this instance.

The Church—I say the Church but I mean the male church—is

rather shy in the presence of women, even as the God of scripture is rather shy of women. God will make a bond of friendship with a hairy patriarch. God interferes with Sarah through her husband. God courts Mary by an angel.

And yet the God of intention entered history through a woman's body (reversing the eye of the needle). The Church, as she exists, is a feminine act, intuition, and pronoun: The Christian Church is the sentimental branch of human theology. (I mean that as praise.) The Church watches the progress of Jesus with the same sense of his heartbreaking failure as did the mother who bore him. In John's account of the wedding at Cana, Mary might be played with maximum flibberty-jibbertry by Maggie Smith. Jesus struggles to extricate his legs from the banquet table in the courtyard; his companions can't help sniggering a bit. The first showing of Jesus's power over Nature, the changing of water into wine, makes no clear theological sense. But as the first Comic Mystery, the scene makes perfect domestic sense. Jesus is instructed by his mother.

### 5. The Sisters of Mercy

I would never in a million years have thought of lobbing a "darling" Franz Schurmann's way, though Franz and I had lunch almost every week for twenty years. Now I wish I had, for Franz would have sluiced the noun through the brines of several tongues, finally cracking its nacreous shell. He would have told me something interesting. Or he would have spit the noun onto his bone plate as something the Chinese have no word for, no use for. (The Chinese tongue had become Franz's point of view.)

Not that Franz was unsophisticated or unacquainted with theatricality. As a young man at Harvard, Franz was the best friend of Bertolt Brecht's son. Franz spent several summers living among the colony of European expatriots in Santa Monica, with Brecht and Weigel and Mann and Isherwood.

After Harvard, Franz embarked on a Pashto-idyll, playing the scholar-gypsy to the hilt: two years on horseback through the Khyber Pass on an anthropological search for some remnant of a lost tribe of blue eyes.

When Franz passed through the molars and incisors of remote mountain villages, he was often invited to share a meal with the bearded men who squatted near a fire. The women who had prepared the meal stood several yards away, watching and waiting for the men to finish, for the men to pluck the remnants of food from their beards.

Franz caught a young woman's eye. She held his glance for only a moment before she spat on the ground and looked away, over her shoulder.

The women who educated me—Catholic nuns belonging to the Irish order of the Sisters of Mercy—looked very much like Franz's Afghan village women. They wore veils, long skirts, long sleeves, laced black shoes—Balenciagas all.

Of the many orders of Catholic nuns founded in nineteenth-century Europe, the majority were not cloistered orders but missionary orders—nursing and teaching orders. Often the founders of such congregations came from upper-middle-class families, but most of the women who swelled the ranks of missionary orders had left peat-fumed, sour-stomached, skinny-cat childhoods behind. They became the least-sequestered women imaginable.

It was in the nineteenth century, too, that secular women in Europe and North America formed suffrage movements, following in the footsteps of missionary nuns and Protestant missionary women. Curiously, it was the burqa-like habits nuns wore—proclaiming their vows of celibacy—that lent them protection in the roustabout world, also a bit of a romantic air.

When seven Irish Sisters of Mercy (the oldest twenty-five) disembarked in San Francisco in December of 1854, they found a city filled with dispirited young men and women who had followed the legend of gold. The Sisters of Mercy spent their first night in California huddled together in St. Patrick's Church on Mission Street; they had no other accommodation. In the morning, and for months afterward, the sisters searched among the wharves and alleys of San Francisco, ministering to men, women, and children they found sleeping in doorways.

The *Christian Advocate,* an anti-Catholic newspaper, published calumny about the nuns; the paper declared them to be women of low repute and opined they should move on—nobody wanted them in San Francisco.

In 1855 the Sisters of Mercy nursed San Franciscans through a cholera outbreak. In 1868 the nuns cared for the victims of a smallpox epidemic. In 1906, after the great earthquake and fire, the Sisters of Mercy set up a tent hospital in the Presidio; they evacuated hundreds of the sick and elderly to Oakland across the Bay. City officials in the nineteenth century invited all religious orders to ride San Francisco's trolleys and cable cars free of charge because of the city's gratitude to the Sisters of Mercy.

As they had done in Ireland, the Sisters of Mercy opened orphanages, schools, and hospitals in California and throughout the United States. By the time our American mothers caught up with the nuns in the 1960s—with the possibility of women living fulfilling lives, independent of family or marriage—the nuns had discarded their black robes in favor of sober pedestrian attire. Vocation has nothing to do with dress-up.

Veiled women were seldom thereafter seen on the streets of America or in European cities, not until the influx of immigrant Muslim women from North Africa and the Middle East in the 1980s.

A shadow of scandal now attaches in Ireland to the founding order of the Sisters of Mercy. An Irish government report released in 2009 documents decades of cruelty perpetrated particularly upon children of the working class in orphanages and homes for unwed mothers run by the Sisters of Mercy. One cannot doubt or excuse the record. The record stands.

The Sisters of Mercy of the Americas—the women I revere— are fewer and older. The great years of the order seem to have passed, but the Sisters continue their ministry to the elderly, to immigrants, to the poor. The Sisters are preparing for a future the rest of us have not yet fully comprehended—a world of increasing poverty and misery—even as they prepare for their absence from the close of the twenty-first century.

Nuns will not entirely disappear from San Francisco as long as we may occasionally glimpse a black mustache beneath a fluttering veil. The Sisters of Perpetual Indulgence is an order of gay drag nuns whose vocation is dress-up.

Like the Sisters of Mercy in early California, the Sisters of Perpetual Indulgence took up their mission in bad repute. Unlike the Sisters of Mercy, the Sisters of P.I. have done everything in their power to maintain a bad repute.

They have their detractors. I was one. I wrote against them because I saw them as mocking heroic lives. Thirty years ago I had lunch with Jack Fertig, aka Sister Boom Boom, in a taqueria on Mission Street. He arrived wearing jeans and a T-shirt. On the wall at the rear of the restaurant was a crucifix—not, I assumed, ironic. The nun in mufti approached the crucifix and fell to his knees. He blessed himself; he bowed his head. Whether this was done for my benefit I don't know. There was no follow-up, no smirk, no sheepishness, no further demonstration of piety. I did not question him about it; I was astonished. But, as I say, I wasn't taken in.

Before he died, Jack Fertig converted to Islam.

A few years ago, I stood on a street corner in the Castro District; I watched as two or three Sisters of P.I. collected money in a coffee can for one of their charities. Their regalia looked haphazard on that day—jeans and tennis shoes beneath their skirts, like altar boys. I couldn't help but admire how the louche nuns encouraged and cajoled the young men and women who approached. The Sisters' catechism involved sexual precaution, drug safety, with plenty of trash repartee so as not to spook their lambs: "Do you have a boyfriend, honey? Are you getting enough to eat? Where do you sleep? Are you compliant with your meds?"

I experienced something like a conversion: Those men are ministering on a street corner to homeless teenagers, and they are pretty good at it. No sooner had I applied the word "good" than I knew it was the right word. Those men are good.

The Sisters of Perpetual Indulgence do what nuns have always done: They heal; they protect; they campaign for social justice; they perform works of charity. The Sisters of Perpetual Indulgence have an additional mission: They scandalize.

For example, on Easter Sundays, the Sisters host the "Hunky Jesus Contest" in Dolores Park. The Sisters and their congregation seem only to be interested in satirizing the trappings of S&M already available in Roman Catholic iconography. (One cannot mock a crucifixion; crucifixion is itself mockery.)

I do not believe the Sisters of Perpetual Indulgence are enemies of the Church; I believe they are a renegade church of true vocation. They are scourges; they are jesters. Their enemy is hypocrisy. In a way, they are as dependent upon the Church as I am. They are as dependent on the nun in a brown wool suit as I am. Without the Church, without the nun, they would make no sense at all.

### 6. The Gray Cat

My father grew up an orphan. The extent of his patriarchy was his sense of responsibility to our family. He otherwise observed no particular rules or rites of masculinity beyond self-possession, and he imposed none beyond respect for our mother. My father was mild and bemused, never touching but lightly, as a child will pet a cat. While our two older siblings had proper names at home, I was "boy" in direct address by my father and "the boy" when I attracted some notice in the third person. Helen was "the girl." Our home was entrusted (in the prayers of our parents) to the care of the Virgin of Guadalupe, and we all rather liked it that way.

Outside the Rodriguez home, God made covenants with men. Covenants were cut out of the male organ. A miasma of psychological fear—fear of smite, fear of flinty tools, fear of lightning— crackled in God's wake. Scripture began to smell of anger—a civet smell. Scripture began to taste of blood—of iron, of salt. I associated heavy, dangerous elements with fathers, with men, but not with my own father.

When I was a child we had a cat. The cat had kittens. She hid them in the shed. The Father Cat, as we called an indolent wild gray, searched for and found the kittens; he smelled them, I guess, or he heard them mewing. He entered the shed. He carried the kittens away in his mouth, one by one, to kill them. I saw the Father Cat flee the shed with a kitten in his soft mouth. I yelled Stop!

I threw a clod of dirt at him. He would not stop, could not; he looked confused, utterly overruled by his natural compulsion. His eyes were terrible; they were not his normal eyes. They were fixed in jealousy—pulled back, as if by some invisible hand at the nape of his neck. That was the name the child's imagination branded him with: The Jealous Cat. He came again. Even after my mother came out to shoo him away with a broom, he loitered at the edge of the yard, biding his time, withstanding the barrage of clods exploding on the wooden fence.

I see dependable Everett Fox (*The Five Books of Moses*) has wondered before me, as thousands before him have wondered, about a "bizarre episode" in *Exodus:* Yahweh divulges to Moses the mission Yahweh has chosen him for. Moses is to return to Egypt and, once in the presence of Pharaoh, is to demand the release of the Israelites in Yahweh's name. Moses accepts Yahweh's command with great trepidation and every excuse in the book—but accepts. So Moses with his wife and sons begins his journey to Egypt. In the desert, at night, Yahweh finds Moses in his tent and seeks to kill him! Moses's wife takes up a flint and cuts off her son's foreskin; she touches the foreskin to Moses's legs and says: "Indeed, a bridegroom of blood are you to me!" Whereupon Yahweh releases Moses.

Everett Fox cites the great rabbi, Martin Buber, who explains this passage (in Fox's capitulation) as "an event that sometimes occurs in hero stories: The deity appears as divine demon and threatens the hero's life. Perhaps this underlines the dangerous side of contact between the human and the divine." Fox explicates the passage further as a prefiguring of the blood smeared on the door lintels of the Israelites during the tenth Egyptian plague.

I can only think of the hormonally conflicted gray cat.

I read an article recently about a medical study that traced a decline in levels of testosterone among new fathers, if those fathers were intimately involved in their infants' care—feeding, holding, changing. Thus does Nurture attempt to vanquish the gray cat.

In Hebrew scripture there is no more valuable signifier than male seed. It is the mucilage of Yahweh's blessing. It is the particulate matter of immeasurable proportion, of metaphor: *as many as, as numerous as* . . . It is the promise of the future. You will hold the desert land by your seed. Multiply, be fruitful, is the overarching instruction. Important kings and prophets come of very bad conceptions. Seed is God's intention, however scattered.

But now it is the twenty-first century and the mitered, bearded, fringed holy men have cast women as gray cats. Destroyers of seed.

### 7. Daddy and Papa

"He" is the default setting in scripture—Jewish, Christian, Islamic. The perception, the preference, the scriptural signifier, the awe of the desert religions, is of a male God. Father. Abba. Lord. Jesus refers to God always as Father, though he insists that God is spirit. Yahweh is unnameable but for the name He (as I was going to write) gives Himself: *I Am*. There is no "He" in *I Am*. The theologian John L. McKenzie proposes (*The Two-Edged Sword*) that a more accurate translation of the holy name might be: "He brings into being." Bringing into being was a potency that the prophets, the evangelists, the compilers of scripture, conceived anthropomorphically as male.

In the desert cultures of the Middle East, religious communities regard homosexual acts as abominations—unnatural, illegal, unclean. But homosexual behavior does not preclude marriage or fatherhood. The notion of a homosexual identity is a comic impossibility. What alone confers an appropriate sexual identity on the male is fatherhood.

Two young men fussing over a baby girl in a stroller. You were not charmed. You said no straight man would make that kind of fuss.

No straight woman, either, Darling.

The new gay stereotype is domestic, childrearing—homosexuals willing to marry at a time when the heterosexual inclination is to dispense with marriage.

Divorce rates in the United States and Europe suggest that women are not happy with the relationships they have with men, and vice versa. And whatever that unhappiness is, I really don't think gay people are the cause. On the other hand, whatever is wrong with heterosexual marriage does have some implication for homosexuals.

The majority of American women are living without spouses. My optimism regarding that tabulation is that a majority of boys in America will grow up assuming that women are strong. My worry is that as so many men absent themselves from the lives of the children they father, boys and girls will grow up without a sense of the tenderness of men.

The prospect of a generation of American children being raised by women in homes without fathers is challenging for religious institutions whose central conception of deity is father, whose central conception of church is family, whose only conception of family is heterosexual. A woman who can do without a husband can do without any patriarchal authority. The oblique remedy some religious institutions propose for the breakdown of heterosexual relationships is a legal objection to homosexual marriages by defining marriage as between one man and one woman.

The gay counteroffensive to the religious argument is (the

American impulse) to seek an African American analogy to homosexual persecution, to claim some historical equivalence to the government-sanctioned persecution of African Americans over centuries. Many African American churches take offense to that particular tack. From the pulpit, the argument sounds something like: We didn't choose our race; homosexuals choose their lifestyle.

I believe there is a valid analogy to be drawn between the legal persecution of homosexuality and the legal persecution of miscegenation—both "crimes against Nature." But the course more comparable to the gay rights movement is the feminist movement, dating to the nineteenth century.

Suffragettes withstood condemnation from every institution of their lives, condemnation that employed the adjectives of unnatural aspiration, adjectives such as "thwarted," "hysterical," "strident," "shrill." Still, it was the brave suffragette (and not the tragic peacock Oscar Wilde) who rescued my sexuality.

In the twentieth century, gays emerging from the closet were beneficiaries of the desire of women to define themselves outside the familial structure. The feminist movement became inclusive not only of wives, mothers, and unmarried women but also of lesbians, and thus, by extension of nonfamilial sisterhood, of homosexual men, of the transgendered, of the eight-legged acronym, LGBT.

A generation ago feminists came up with "Ms." as a titular designation of gender not based upon marital status or age. Ms. was no sooner on offer than most women I know and most institutions gratefully adopted it. Ms. transported the woman signified out the door and into public life, independent of cultural surmise.

Using the homeliest of metaphors—coming out of the kitchen;

coming out of the closet—heterosexual women and homosexuals announced, just by being themselves without apology, the necessity of a reordered civil society. We are—women and homosexuals are— for however long I don't know, dispensed (by constitutional laws, state laws) from having to fit into heterosexual roles and heterosexual social patterns that have been upheld for so long by reference to "the natural law." Natural law, as cited against sodomy, against abortion, against birth control, against miscegenation, is neither exactly the "natural moral law," which is a philosophical construct—the understanding placed in us by God at the creation— nor exactly the law of Nature; that is, how Nature works. Rather, it is a value placed upon behavior by someone or some agency, most often with reference to some divinely inspired statutory text, that denounces or declares illegal or punishable any deviation from what the authority or the text declares to be natural human behavior. Boys will be boys and girls like glitter.

I know there are some homosexuals who see the gay couples in line for marriage licenses, or filling out forms for adoption, or posing for wedding announcements in the *New York Times,* as antithetical to an ancient culture of refusal that made the best of a short story—of youth and chance and public toilets and then the long half-life of irony and discretion.

There certainly are homosexuals of my generation who never dared hope for a novel of marriage but only one of renunciation. E. M. Forster imagined a marriage novel, but then stipulated it not be published during his lifetime. The Church regards homosexual marriage as a travesty that will promote the undoing of marriage. But I propose the single mother is a greater threat to the patriarchal determination of what constitutes a natural order.

I am thinking of David Grossman, the Israeli novelist, who, in a profile in the *New Yorker*, said: "If God came to Sarah and told her, 'Give me your son, your only one, your beloved, Isaac,' she will tell him, 'Give me a break,' not to say 'Fuck off.'"

I am thinking of the Mormon mother who told me on Temple Square in Salt Lake City: "The Church teaches us that family is everything. And then the Church tells me that I should abandon my homosexual son. I will not do it!"

It is clear to me that civic attitudes toward homosexuality and gay marriage are changing. In countries we loosely describe as Western, opinion polls and secular courts are deciding in favor of the legalization of gay marriage. Nevertheless, the desert religions will stand opposed to homosexuality, to homosexual acts, unless the desert religions turn to regard the authority of women. And that will not happen until the desert religions reevaluate the meaning of women. And that will not happen until the desert religions see "bringing into being" is not a power we should call male only. And that will not happen until the desert religions see the woman as father, the father as woman, indistinguishable in authority and creative potence.

My place in the Church depends upon you, Darling.

### 8. The Sultan's Wives

But you're right, of course.

"Darling" is a feeble impulse to cover some essential embarrassment in my situation. In my life, I should say. Will I be bringing a spouse, for example. Well, that depends, doesn't it?

It is the queer lexicon that is behind the times now. Is my partner a husband? Is my husband a partner? We are not a law firm. Is my partner my "friend," a wreath of quotation marks orbiting his head? Lover sounds sly. Boyfriend sounds fleeting. Husband sounds wistful.

This might amuse you, Darling, now that you are dead. It wouldn't have . . . well, maybe it would have. In the dawn of a warm spring morning, the road to Jerusalem was shrouded in fog. Jimmy and I arrived at the American Colony Hotel. The Palestinian clerk looked at me, looked at Jimmy. The clerk said there was a problem with our reservation. The problem was that the suite we had reserved—all the suites, in fact—had only one bed.

That's no problem, I said. (I was annoyed with myself; I had asked friends who know Jerusalem well if there would be a problem about our sharing a room. And I had been assured there would not be a problem.)

For the desk clerk, there was a problem.

In a previous life, this wonderful hotel had been the palace of an Ottoman sultan whose several wives were salted away in various rooms that still surround the courtyard; Begum Monday next door to Begum Tuesday, and so on. Now suites.

Ah! The reservation clerk seized upon a solution; he even dinged his little bell.

Please, if we would care to take a little breakfast on the patio, he would see to our room.

After we had finished with breakfast, the clerk led us up a staircase to our room, and voilà: A cot was unfolded and was being made up as a daybed by a middle-aged Palestinian man whose sensibility we were conspiring to protect. The Palestinian man finished smoothing the coverlet then he stood back from the cot. He turned to us, where we stood in the doorway. He smiled. He winked!

Q: Why do I stay in the Catholic Church?

A: I stay in the Church because the Church is more than its

ignorance; the Church gives me more than it denies me. I stay in the Church because it is mine.

I meant what I said to the nun: I will stay as long as she does. I may even stay longer. The Church and I have the same dilemma, really. To wit: "Tradition has always declared that 'homosexual acts are intrinsically disordered.' [CDF, *Persona humana* 8.] They are contrary to the natural law. They close the sexual act to the gift of life. They do not proceed from a genuine affective and sexual complementarity. Under no circumstances can they be approved." (*Catechism of the Catholic Church*, second edition, copyright 2001. United States Conference of Catholic Bishops. Libreria Editrice Vaticana.)

I can walk away from the bishops' formulation of my "intrinsic" disorder, but the Church cannot walk away from the bishops' formulation, even though some within the Church may be sympathetic toward homosexuals. I know this is supremely boring to non-queers and non-Catholics and readers of Faulkner, but stay a moment and then we will go to Costco. Sexual complementarity is not, obviously, insurmountable, or there would be no problem. I will object with my last breath, however, to anyone denying "genuine affective complementarity" to queers. I would not deny "genuine affective complementarity" to a dog. Or a cat. Or a parakeet. (My aunt had a parakeet named Sanchez. They were devoted to each other.) Or to an apostle.

At the time I write this, the only institution on earth that recognizes my ability to love is Costco. On the Costco registry, I have a spouse.

What I will not countenance is that the Church denies me the ability to love. That is what "affective complementarity" is: It is love. If that is the Church's position, the Church is in error. Keep the word "marriage." Let marriage mean one man and one woman. (Sanchez died a week after my aunt died.) But I want a word. How about "love"?

We are gathered here, in the sight of the security cameras at Costco, to witness . . .

What are you smiling at, Darling?

### 9. An Angel Hovers over the Garden of Eden

*Can we do something on Sunday? A movie? A walk?*

If not each other's walkers, we were certainly each other's talkers. A professor of mine remarked a good many years ago that the vocal cords are the most reliable, longest-enduring sexual organs. It was the exercise of vocal cords that led us to step over the bodies of our sleeping lovers to drive twenty miles north, to slide into the banquette of the Garden of Eden. A brilliant February morning. A foggy July evening. Your skirt hiked up for driving; your yearly new car.

And you were right, Darling. Going through to the bar was a betrayal, a sudden disinclination for intimacy; boredom with your melancholy; the hope of an early evening. Let's make this an early evening. Darling. Because all of a sudden you were going to say—you did say—that I was pretending to be someone I am not. In fact, Darling, I was pretending to be someone I am. Despite my many sins and shortcuts, I have always been a player—on my mother's side.

A player recognizes other players. I once met a German shepherd who was a player. And so was his dog. Oh, come on, what's wrong now? What should I call you, then? Sweetie? Dulcinea?

I had studied so diligently to become a serious man. I stood in awe of serious, competent men—scholars, janitors, fathers.

But I had as well, at the time of the Garden of Eden, an adolescent anxiety about Chekhovian Sunday evenings, about melancholy, about sex. I had endeavored to suggest to you, Darling, without resorting to scarves or cigarette holders—you just never cared to notice—that I had some interest in the casbah, in people you wouldn't approve of. Obviously I had a fear of the casbah, as well. One foot in. "Darling" seemed to fit the bill.

Exhibit A: I wore a suit and tie; Helen carried a purse—teenage brother and sister standing on the sidewalk in front of the Curran Theatre in San Francisco. We had lunched at Normandy Lane in the basement of the City of Paris. We had used the restrooms at the St. Francis. The future was years ahead of us. We were still an hour early for the Saturday matinee. We looked at the photographs of the cast. A Yellow Cab pulled up to the curb. The back door opened. Cary Grant got out of the cab. I nudged Helen. Cary Grant extended his arm into the cab and handed out Dyan Cannon, whose portrait we had just examined. (Dyan Cannon was playing the female lead in the national company of *How to Succeed in Business Without Really Trying*.) Cary Grant drew Dyan Cannon into an embrace. Dyan Cannon melted somewhat. Cary Grant kissed Dyan Cannon on her lips. We watched. Cary Grant got back into the cab; he rolled down the window. "Bye-bye, darling," he called as the cab sped away.

I have found that "darling" serves as a signal to women that one's relationship to them is going to be a comic pas, an operetta, a tease. (If that's the signal you caught, Darling, you were not wrong.)

If a woman returns the serve—if she is a willing player—then you've got her where you want her; "darling" is understood: One is not a sexual player. One is Cary Grant. One has Randolph Scott sewing curtains back at the ranch. "Darling" is the net, not the birdie.

You were not going to join my menagerie of darlings, though, were you, Darling? Just trying you out. Sorry.

Elizabeth Taylor, toward the end of her life, when she could (I imagine) have summoned anyone in the world to dine, spent many evenings at a gay club in West Hollywood, just to be a darling among darlings. She was too fond of life, too fond of people, too shrewd to be shrewd, to retire into mystery.

A favorite darling-ist of mine is Harold Bloom. He's not gay, is he? And yet he darlings like a champ.

But the all-time was Bunny Breckinridge. "Hell-o, darling," Bunny would purr, straightening the lapels of his silk suit, composing his hands (diamond ring) as if he were leaning forward upon a walking stick—a top-hatted chorister's stance, a top-hatted chorister's patience. Bunny could sit without moving for long periods of time, like someone on stage, which, of course, he had been—he had been on the stage. Every thirty minutes he would sigh a two-tone sigh like an ormolu clock to let you know that he was still there, that he would wait you out. Bunny's mannerisms were as those described in some bad translation of a Russian masterpiece. He giggled suggestively. He squeaked with pleasure. He winked salaciously. Face powder dusted his collar; his rinsed white hair was swept back to a meringue peak at the North Pole, like the hair of one of those puff-cheeked Aeolian figures in the corners of antique maps.

And Bunny could soliloquize. Picture Edith Evans, seated on a stone bench in a painted garden in some Restoration comedy. Dirtier, of course. He once recounted, for reasons that had to do with a diamond cross he wore at his throat, the Passion and Death of Our Lord Jesus Christ. At the completion of the narrative, huge tears, clotted with powder, rolled down his cheeks. Bunny is the only human being I have ever met for whom the death of Christ had the immediacy of personal tragedy. "He died for our sins, darling," Bunny confided piteously.

**Then you said:** *Why are you telling me all this? If men would only listen to themselves sometimes.*

**I said:** Men? I'm demonstrating the rhetorical uses of "darling"—as if you were my Orals Examiner.

**You:** *Then as your Orals Examiner, Darling, I feel I should tell you something important. "Darling" should be intimate; "darling" should be understood, not flung about the room like a stripper's garter. If you feel you really must darling someone in public, and karaoke is not readily available, scribble your sonnet on a napkin and pass it under the table when no one is looking. Don't toss "darlings" around like you are feeding the seals. It is no way to treat a woman. (Tears.)*

Later that same evening . . .

**You:** *Should we get a room?*

**I:** What? (Punctuation cannot convey.)

**You:** *It's late. We could watch a movie.*

**I:** I think I've seen this movie.

**You:** . . . ? (Judy Garland.)

**I:** . . . ? (Houdini.)

**You:** *You're not interested in women. Say it.*

**Zorba the Greek:** "God has a very big heart, but there is one sin He will not forgive. If a woman calls a man to her bed and he will not go."

I:  I am not interested in sleeping with a woman, if that's what
   you mean. Isn't it odd we say "sleep" when what we
   mean . . .

You:  *Thank you. That is what I mean. Was that so hard?*

I:  Yes.

So, just like that, we were over the rainbow. You would continue to explore the pleasures of the natural law. There was a
young one, a rich one, a dumb one, a tan—probably gay, we both
agreed. And I was free to darling up a storm—a neutered noun
twirling about a neon palm tree.

When the time came, I wasn't sure how I should introduce
you. . . .

Darling, this is Jimmy, I said.

(Your braceleted arm extended.)

Over time, you stopped making faces; over time, my theatrical affection became the emblem of our true affection.

You even returned the herring in kind. In a small white bed, in
a curtained cubicle, the prongs of the slipped oxygen tube hissing
about your throat, you endeavored to show you understood who
was holding your hand. With your eyes closed, you raised one
finger and whispered: *Darling.*

### 10. The Maternity Ward

The maternity wards of Tel Aviv are in a contest with the maternity wards of Ramallah. Might the future depend—as in the Old
Testament—on the number of children your tribe produces? If
Ramallah wins, there will be a Palestinian state. Babies are a political force in the world.

For several years, we, in the West, have talked about the future as a "clash of civilizations," by which we meant primarily a clash between fundamentalists and secular society. The attacks of September 11 seemed to many Americans to join that clash.

September 11 has prompted me to consider the future in terms of a growing, worldwide female argument with the "natural" male doctorate of the beard—a coming battle between men and women.

In China, men outnumber women. That might be the statistic to think about. One outcome of the one-child policy was that many couples contrived to make their one child a son. The result of the policy—the contrivance, the forced abortions, etcetera—is that China prepares for economic, technological, and military preeminence in the twenty-first century, the rare-earth century, the expanding desert century, the starving century, while sustaining a fundamental biological imbalance: There are too few women.

Such an imbalance might seem to favor a patriarchal order by force of number. But because reproduction is such a profound human balance, the rare-woman century may give humans of female gender the opportunity to control, to seize control of, reproduction. If the female gender were ever to control reproduction, then the female gender would control what?

Point of view.

If menses were the parable, not seed—if sea, not ships; if sky, not missiles? If protective imagination were the parable, not domination, not conflict, then . . . ?

If *Silent Night* were the prologue, and not *Sing, Goddess, the anger of Peleus's son.*

Then?

I asked the question of a priest-scholar: If women were to control reproduction, what would women control? The priest paused for a moment before answering efficiently: "Evolution. Who controls the zygote controls the zeitgeist."

It is only after shopping my question around the boys' club that I bring it at last to the banquette of the Garden of Eden.

Here is my question, Darling: Say there is a battle forming between men and women. I do not mean for equality, but for primacy—for who will ultimately control reproduction . . . What are you doing?

*Looking for my pills.*

What's wrong?

*Nothing's wrong. I'm looking for my pills.*

So here's my question. What would a woman control if a woman controlled . . . ?

*A schoolboy's question. Why must it be a question of "control"?*

You haven't even heard the question.

*I heard the frame. It's a riddle, isn't it? No doubt there is a correct answer. Tickle me. Amuse me.*

I asked Father Rafferty the same question. If women control reproduction, what will women control? You know what his answer was?

*I cannot imagine.*

No. His answer was evolution. That's good, isn't it?

*Are there bones in skate?*

So . . . ?

*Look, Richard, a woman . . . No I can't speak for Women. I cannot consider your question abstractly. Your question presses against me like an exploded safety bag. Back up! Or should I say pull out? (Once more to the handbag.) There you are! (She aligns the arrows on the safety cap.) Pregnancy is never a hypothetical for a woman. Never. Not even for me. Not even at my age. Cheers. (Prednisone.) It is a condition of our existence.*

Your answer is you cannot conceive the question?

*No, my dear. My observation is that you cannot conceive! That*

*freedom alone allows you to conceive of conception as a power. Whereas*
*a woman might argue that a refusal to conceive is the only power.*

Are you sure you're not just pulling a hetero on me?

*Women and men will never be equal. Women will always be superior*
*in knowledge and irony because men will never have a clue what it feels*
*like to have the entire dangerous future of the planet crammed up their*
*twats. I'm not pulling a hetero. I'm pulling a utero.*

You are so pleased with your funny that I am rewarded with
your laughter, which is like a percolating calliope. Everyone in the
Garden of Eden must turn to see what sort of creature could pro-
duce such a ridiculous, infectious sound.

### 11. Three Women

A woman:

Andy Warhol made a tracing of Leonardo's *Annunciation.*
Leonardo's painting is venerably burnished—browns, golds, Ve-
netian red. On the left side of Leonardo's canvas is an angel, of
idealized profile—one dead eye and two partially aroused pin-
ions. The angel kneels in the manner of a mezzo-soprano cavalier
and raises its right hand in benediction; its left hand supports the
stalk of a lily.

Mary sits at a reading carrel; her right hand worries the pages
of an open Psalter. In the background are some odd topiary—
cypress, perhaps—and a garden in which lilies bloom. The van-
ishing point is a mountain in the far distance. Mary's lap is
shelf-like—knees apart, feet braced, as is characteristic of many
Annunciation paintings—but not yet receptive to the implication
of the angel's presence.

Warhol's silk-screen rendition, a kind of explication, uses three
colors—gray, salmon, white (in the version I prefer; Warhol
printed several variations)—and crops the scene to a close-up, iso-

lating three elements: On the left, the blessing hand of the angel (the Question, the Proposal). On the right, Mary's hand, restive on the Psalter (the incipient reply, not yet an assent). In the center is the white alp, like a dish of ice cream in a comic book (the Suitor, the Unknowable, the Impossible).

The alp has sent its mouthpiece to ask if it may enter the foreground, overshadow the maiden. Gabriel kneels to proclaim: Hail, Darling, full of grace. The Lord is with thee. Blessed art thou amongst women. And blessed is the fruit of thy womb, Jesus.

"It is *a* woman I want rather than any particular one," the young Victorian novelist, William Makepeace Thackeray, wrote to his mother in frustration.

A woman:

I was crossing Broadway on my way to a theater—a warm spring evening, around seven o'clock, still light. Within the crosswalk, a woman walked alongside me. "Are you visiting New York?" she asked very pleasantly. She was dressed in a creamish, knittish, knockoff Chanel with gold buttons. Forty. Thirty-five, forty. Nice-looking. Not much makeup. Umbrella, just in case. You could tell she was a nice woman, even without the umbrella. "Where are you going in such a hurry?" she asked, trying to keep pace. I'm on my way to the theater, I said. "Would you like some company?" This last she said with desperation; she was cognizant of the absurdity of her question, posed in a crosswalk on Times Square. Oh, no thank you, I said, cognizant of the Greer Garson blitheness of my reply. I'm meeting some friends at the theater. At which her (gloved) hand moved to cover her mouth, stifling a vowel that was sick and sorrowful—humiliation, I thought, at having, on what must surely have been her maiden voyage as a hooker, or nearly, tried it out on a gay man who probably looked as benign to her (my blue suit, perhaps) as she looked to me, and probably I was one of the very few solitary male pedestrians on Broadway who was more interested in seeing a play than in sex with a woman who held an umbrella. I wished her a good evening. Her face crumpled in tears as she turned away to her fate.

You see, I badly needed a "darling" at that moment—to make her smile, even if ruefully; to make it seem we were two adults who knew the score, which we weren't, which we didn't, neither of us.

When William Thackeray died at age fifty-two, a famous author, the most famous English author of his time after Dickens, he left two young daughters and a wife in a sanitarium who suffered from what we would now call postpartum depression. Mrs. Thackeray never recovered but lived a very long time in perplexity, seated in a lawn chair. William Thackeray was buried at Kensal Green Cemetery, London. Several figures in black, famous figures—Penguin paperbacks—accompanied the Thackeray daughters to their father's grave.

But what was that unseemly caterwauling?

Black-clothed figures turned from the open grave to watch the advance of a carriageful of whooping and gesticulating Mayfair tarts in parrot's plumage. The women choired lusty benedictions as their carriage drove round and round the grave: Goodbye Willie, they cried. Toodaloo, Dearie. We had a few laughs, though, didn't we, Darlin'!

A woman:

Jesus of Nazareth is not known for sparing anyone embarrassment, least of all his family, but in his meeting with the Samaritan woman, he displays evidence of knowing the score. As does she. And, as you say, "darling" is understood:

At Jacob's Well. Noon. Jesus rests from a long journey on foot. His friends have gone into town to look for something to eat. A woman approaches the well. She carries a clay jar. Jesus says to the woman, Will you give me something to drink?

*Wait, a Jew is asking a Samaritan for a drink?*

If you only knew what God was giving you right this minute . . .

*I don't see your water-skin, love.*

. . . you'd be the one asking for a drink.

*You can't drink from mine, though, can you? Defile your inner temple, outer temple, which is it? And the well is deep, trust me. How do you propose to draw water without a skin?*

Whoever drinks your water will soon be thirsty again.

*If you're afraid of the trots, you should stick to your own well.*

No one who drinks the water I give will ever be thirsty again. The water I pour out will become a spring of life.

*Oh, well then. In that case* (as she lowers her leather bag into the well)—*a skin of my donkey-swill for a drop of your kosher magic.* (She extends the dripping water bag to Jesus.)

Call your husband.

*What's that got to do . . . hey!* (Snatching back the water bag, splashing them both.) *I don't have a husband.*

You got that one right (Darling); you've had four husbands and counting. But the one you've got now isn't your husband.

*Oh, a prophet, too! Should've known from the toenails. My ancestors worshipped on this mountain a long time before you people showed up.*

The hour is coming when you will worship the Father neither on this mountain nor in Jerusalem.

*Oh, Jerusalem. I was forgetting: True worship only happens in Jerusalem.*

You worship what you don't know. We worship what we know; salvation comes from the Jews. But the hour is coming—it is already here—when true worshippers will worship the Father in spirit and truth. That is the worship the Father wants.

*Well* (Darling), *when the Messiah comes, I'm sure he will explain everything to everyone. Even hillbillies like me.*

You're talking to him.

## 12. Mystery

You were raised Catholic. You said you didn't believe. Much anyway. How one lives one's life is what one believes, you said. You admitted to downright needing Christmas.

And music. Twice you said you didn't know if you assented to the notion of God.

Notion? Existence then. You said you believed in mystery. Mystery? You said religion—any religion you knew about—was a cult of patriarchy. Men in the Bible were better fathers than husbands, you noticed.

A friend who sat with you through the night, one of the worst nights, very near the end, recounted to me how troubled you seemed. *What a bad person I've been,* you said to the friend, to the shadows, to the statues huddled in the shadows (*Wait, are those statues?*), turning your face away. *What a poor mother, what a poor daughter.*

No, no, the friend reassured: Come on, you are a very good mother, your children are wonderful. They adore you. Everyone adores you.

I am thinking of your two-hour theorem, Darling. It is the most fortifying advice I have ever received. You said: I find I can stand anything for two hours. Fly through a thunderstorm. Drive through a desert. Visit a kid in prison. Root canal. Cocktail party in Brentwood. Birth. Financial report. Roast turkey. Just do it and don't fret! Think about getting home. Think about pulling into the driveway. Think about cereal and bananas.

In the morning, your friend said, you opened your eyes, though no one could enter them; you spoke as if from a trance. *How wonderful God is,* you said. *How beautiful it is!*

I mean, who doesn't love the breast, the throat, the hands, the rings, the laughter? Who doesn't love the economy of her ways? Her sudden abandonment to joy? The way she can arrange a bed, a sheet, a blanket, a pillow. The way she can leave everything better than when she entered.

I know plenty of men who can arrange a room. But I am not talking about "taste," I am talking about . . . Partly, it is the patience for folding material—the patience of square corners. But partly it is the carelessness of allowable drift. Of opening a window and closing a curtain and letting the curtain blow as it will.

During World War II, the U.S. military, in an attempt to make men more uniform, studied the art of the hospital, the convent, the feminine. Men were trained to make up their cots in an efficient, spotless, feminine way. Selfless, in other words—literally selfless, as a grave is selfless. One bed must be exactly like the next. Inspecting officers tended to make a metrical fetish of a made bed, a punishment of what should promise ease.

Darling, you couldn't wrap a package to save your soul. I watched as you taped together some wrinkled, flowered, saved remnant of Mother's Day. Then you tied on a wide plaid ribbon. The result was not perfection. It was pretty. Same with your flower arrangements—plunking a fistful of cut flowers into a vase, any vase, any flowers. One would need to study for years to achieve the carelessness of your impulse. An unkempt, Pre-Raphaelite prettiness followed you wherever you went, and I don't understand at all how you came by it. I don't even understand what it was.

Who doesn't love her stockings?

You were dead, so you missed the plump-jowled televangelist Jerry Falwell confiding to the gaunt-jowled televangelist Pat Robertson that the Islamist attack on America was the result not of religious extremism but of divine displeasure with a morally decadent United States of America: *"I really believe that the pagans, and the abortionists, and the feminists, and the gays and the lesbians who are actively trying to make that an alternative lifestyle, the ACLU, the People For the American Way, all of them who have tried to secularize America. I point the finger in their face and say, 'You helped this happen.'"*

He means us, Darling. You and me in the bar of the Garden of Eden, passing those long-past afternoons.

I cannot imagine my freedom as a homosexual man without women in veils. Women in red Chanel. Women in flannel nightgowns. Women in their mirrors. Women saying, Honey-bunny. Women saying, We'll see. Women saying, If you lay one hand on that child, I swear to God I will kill you. Women in curlers. Women in high heels. Younger sisters, older sisters; women and girls. Without women.

Without you.

# six

# Saint Cesar of Delano

The funeral for Cesar Chavez took place in an open field near Delano, a small agricultural town at the southern end of California's Central Valley. I remember an amiable Mexican disorder, the crowd listening and not listening to speeches and prayers delivered from a raised platform beneath a canvas tent. I do not remember a crowd numbering thirty thousand or fifty thousand, as some estimates have it—but then I do not remember. Perhaps a cool, perhaps a warm, spring sun. Men in white shirts carried forward a pine box. The ease of their movement suggested the lightness of their burden.

When Cesar Chavez died in his sleep in 1993, not yet a very old man at sixty-six, he died—as he had so often portrayed himself in life—as a loser. The United Farm Workers (UFW) union he had cofounded was in decline; the union had five thousand members, equivalent to the population of one small Central Valley town. The labor in California's agricultural fields was largely taken up by Mexican migrant workers—the very workers Chavez had been unable to reconcile to his American union; the workers he had branded as "scabs."

I went to the funeral because I was writing a piece on Chavez for the *Los Angeles Times*. It occurs to me now that I was present at a number of events involving Cesar Chavez. I was at the edge of the crowd in 1966, when Chavez led UFW marchers to the steps of the capitol in Sacramento to rally support for a strike against grape growers. I went to hear Chavez speak at Stanford University. I can recall everything about the occasion except why I was there. I stood at the back. I remember a light of late afternoon among the oaks beyond the plate-glass windows of Tresidder Union; I remember the Reverend Robert McAfee Brown introducing Cesar Chavez. Something about Chavez embarrassed me— embarrassed me in the way I would be embarrassed if someone from my family had turned up at Stanford in a dream to lecture undergraduates on the hardness of a Mexican's life. I did not join in the standing ovation. Well, I was already standing. I wouldn't give him anything. And yet, of course, there was something compelling about his homeliness.

In her thoroughly researched and thoroughly unsentimental book *The Union of Their Dreams: Power, Hope, and Struggle in Cesar Chavez's Farm Worker Movement*, journalist Miriam Pawel chronicles the lives of a collection of people—farm workers, idealistic college students, young lawyers from the East Coast, a Presbyterian minister, and others—who gave years of their lives at subsistence pay to work for the UFW. Every person Pawel profiles has left the union—has been fired or has quit in disgust or frustration. Nevertheless, it is not beside the point to notice that Cesar Chavez inspired such a disparate, devoted company.

We forget that the era we call the sixties was not only a time of vast civic disaffection; it was also a time of religious idealism. At the forefront of what amounted to the religious revival of America in those years were the black Protestant ministers of the civil rights movement, ministers who insisted upon a moral dimension to the rituals of everyday American life—eating at a lunch counter, riding a bus, going to school.

Cesar Chavez similarly cast his campaign for better wages and living conditions for farm workers as a religious movement. He became for many Americans, especially Mexican Americans (my parents among them), a figure of spiritual authority. I remember a small brown man with an Indian aspect leading labor protests that were also medieval religious processions of women, children, nuns, students, burnt old men, under the banner of Our Lady of Guadalupe.

By the time Chavez had become the most famous Mexican American anyone could name—his face on the cover of *Time*— the majority of Mexican Americans lived in cities, far from the tragic fields of California's Central Valley that John Steinbeck had made famous a generation earlier. Mexican Americans were more likely to work in construction or in service-sector jobs than in the fields.

Cesar Chavez was born in Yuma, Arizona, in 1927. During the years of his hardscrabble youth, he put away his ambitions for college. He gave his body to the fields in order to keep his mother from having to work in the fields. The young farm worker accumulated an autodidact's library—books on economics, philosophy, history. (Years later, Chavez was apt to quote Winston Churchill at UFW staff meetings.) He studied the black civil rights movement, particularly the writings of Martin Luther King Jr. He studied most intently the lives and precepts of Saint Francis of Assisi and Mohandas Gandhi.

It is heartening to learn about private acts of goodness in notorious lives. It is discouraging to learn of the moral failures of famously good people. The former console. But to learn that the Reverend Martin Luther King Jr. was a womanizer is to be confronted with the knowledge that flesh is a complicated medium for grace. To learn that there were flaws in the character of Cesar Chavez is again to wonder at the meaning of a good life. During his lifetime, Chavez was considered by many to be a saint. Pawel is writing outside the hagiography, but while reading her book I could not avoid thinking about the nature of sanctity.

Saints? Holiness? I apologize for introducing radiant nouns.

Cesar Chavez modeled his life on the lives of the saints—an uncommon ambition in a celebrated American life. In America, influence is the point of prominence; power over history is the point. I think Cesar Chavez would have said striving to lead a holy life is the point—a life lived in imitation of Jesus Christ, the most famous loser on a planet spilling over with losers. The question is whether the Mexican saint survives the tale of the compromised American hero.

The first portrait in *The Union of Their Dreams* is of Eliseo Medina. At the advent of the UFW, Eliseo was a shy teenager, educated only through the eighth grade. Though he was not confident in English, Medina loved to read *El Malcriado,* the feisty bilingual weekly published by the UFW. Eliseo Medina remembered how his life changed on a Thursday evening when he went to hear Chavez in the social hall of Our Lady of Guadalupe Church in Delano. Medina was initially "disappointed by the leader's unimpressive appearance." But by the end of the meeting, he had determined to join the union.

No Chavez speech I have read or heard approaches the rhetorical brilliance of the Protestant ministers of the black civil rights movement. Chavez was, however, brilliantly theatrical. He seemed to understand, the way Charlie Chaplin understood, how to make an embarrassment of himself—his mulishness, his silence, his witness. His presence at the edge of a field was a blight of beatitude.

Chavez studied the power of abstinence. He internalized his resistance to injustice by refusing to eat. What else can a poor man do? Though Chavez had little success encouraging UFW volunteers to follow the example of his abstinence, he was able to convince millions of Americans (as many as twenty million by some estimates) not to buy grapes or lettuce.

Farmers in the Central Valley were bewildered to find themselves roped into a religious parable. Indeed, Valley growers, many of them Catholics, were dismayed when their children came home from parochial schools and reported that Chavez was upheld as a moral exemplum in religion class.

At a time in the history of American business when Avis saw the advantage of advertising itself as "Number Two" and Volkswagen sold itself as "the Bug," Chavez made the smallness of his union, even the haphazardness of it, a kind of boast. In 1968, during his most publicized fast to support the strike of grape pickers, Chavez issued this statement (he was too weak to read aloud): "Those who oppose our cause are rich and powerful and they have many allies in high places. We are poor. Our allies are few."

Chavez broke his 1968 fast with a public relations tableau that was rich with symbol and irony. Physically diminished (in photographs his body looks to be incapable of sustaining an erect, seated position), Chavez was handed bread (sacramental ministration after his trial in the desert) by Chris Hartmire, the Presbyterian minister who gave so much of his life to serving Chavez and his union. Alongside Chavez sat Robert F. Kennedy, then a U.S. senator from New York. The poor and the meek also have allies in high places.

Here began a conflict between deprivation and success that would bedevil Chavez through three decades. In a way, this was a struggle between the Mexican Cesar Chavez and the American Cesar Chavez. For it was Mexico that taught Chavez to value a life of suffering. It was America that taught him to fight the causes of suffering.

The speech Chavez wrote during his hunger strike of 1968 (wherein he likened the UFW to David fighting the Goliath of agribusiness) announced the Mexican theme: "I am convinced that the truest act of courage, the strongest act of manliness is to sacrifice ourselves for others in a totally non-violent struggle for justice. To be a man is to suffer for others. God help us to be men." (Nearly three decades later, in the program for Chavez's funeral, the wording of his psalm would be revised—"humanity" substituted for "manliness": *To be human is to suffer for others. God help me to be human*.)

Nothing else Chavez wrote during his life had such haunting power for me as that public prayer for a life of suffering; no utterance sounded so Mexican. Other cultures in the world assume the reality of suffering as something to be overcome. Mexico assumes the inevitability of suffering. That knowledge informs the folk music of Mexico, the bitter humor of Mexican proverb. To be a man is to suffer for others—you're going to suffer anyway. The code of *machismo* (which American English has translated too crudely as sexual bravado) in Mexico derives from a medieval chivalry whereby a man uses his strength or his resolve or even his foolishness (as did Don Quixote) to protect those less powerful. God help us to be men.

Mexicans believe that in 1531 the Virgin Mary appeared in brown skin, in royal Aztec raiment, to a converted Indian peasant named Juan Diego. The Virgin asked that a church be erected on the site of her four apparitions in order that Mexican Indians could come to her and tell her of their suffering. The image of Our Lady of Guadalupe was an aspect of witness at every UFW demonstration.

Though he grew up during the American Depression, Cesar Chavez breathed American optimism and American activism. In the early 1950s, while still a farm worker, he met Fred Ross of the Community Service Organization, a group inspired by the principles of the radical organizer Saul Alinsky. Chavez later became an official in the CSO, and eventually its president. He persuaded notoriously apathetic Mexican Americans to register to vote by encouraging them to believe they could change their lives in America.

If you would understand the tension between Mexico and the United States that is playing out along our mutual border, you must understand the psychic tension between Mexican stoicism— if that is a rich enough word for it—and American optimism. On the one side, the Mexican side, Mexican peasants are tantalized by the American possibility of change. On the other side, the American side, the tyranny of American optimism has driven Americans to neurosis and depression, when the dream is elusive or less meaningful than the myth promised. This constitutes the great irony of the Mexican-American border: American sadness has transformed the drug lords of Mexico into billionaires, even as the peasants of Mexico scramble through the darkness to find the American dream.

By the late 1960s, as the first UFW contracts were being signed, Chavez began to brood. Had he spent his poor life only to create a middle class? Lionel Steinberg, the first grape grower to sign with the UFW, was drawn by Chavez's charisma but chagrined at the union's disordered operations. Steinberg wondered: "Is it a social movement or a trade union?" He urged Chavez to use experienced negotiators from the AFL-CIO.

Chavez paid himself an annual wage of $5,000. "You can't change anything if you want to hold on to a good job, a good way of life, and avoid suffering." The world-famous labor leader would regularly complain to his poorly paid staff about the phone bills

they ran up and about what he saw as the misuse of a fleet of sec-
ondhand UFW cars. He held the union hostage to the purity of
his intent. Eliseo Medina, who had become one of the union's
most effective organizers, could barely support his young family;
he asked Chavez about setting up a trust fund for his infant son.
Chavez promised to get back to him but never did. Eventually,
thoroughly discouraged by the mismanagement of the union,
Medina resigned.

In 1975 Chavez helped to initiate legislation that prohibited the
use of the short-handled hoe in the fields—its two-foot-long haft
forced farm workers to stoop all day. That achievement would
outlast the decline of his union. By the early 1970s, California vegetable growers began signing sweetheart contracts with the rival
Teamsters Union. The UFW became mired in scraps with un-
friendly politicians in Sacramento. Chavez's attention wandered.
He imagined a "Poor Peoples Union" that would reach out to senior citizens and people on welfare. He contacted church officials
within the Vatican about the possibility of establishing a lay religious society devoted to service to the poor. Chavez became interested in the Hutterite communities of North America and the
Israeli kibbutzim as possible models for such a society.

Chavez visited Synanon, the drug-rehabilitation commune
headed by Charles Dederich, shortly before some Synanon members were implicated in a series of sexual scandals and criminal
assaults. Chavez borrowed from Synanon a version of a disciplin-
ary practice called the Game, whereby UFW staff members were
obliged to stand in the middle of a circle of peers and submit to
fierce criticism. Someone sympathetic to Chavez might argue that
the Game was an inversion of an ancient monastic discipline
meant to teach humility. Someone less sympathetic might con-

clude that Chavez was turning into a petty tyrant. I think both estimations are true.

From his reading, Chavez would have known that Saint Francis of Assisi desired to imitate the life of Jesus. The followers of Francis desired to imitate the life of Francis. Within ten years of undertaking his mendicant life, Francis had more than one thousand followers. Francis realized he could not administer a growing religious order by personal example. He relinquished the administration of the Franciscans to men who had some talent for organization. Cesar Chavez never gave up his position as head of the UFW.

In 1977 Chavez traveled to Manila as a guest of President Ferdinand Marcos. He ended up praising the old dictator. There were darker problems within the UFW. There were rumors that some within the inner circle were responsible for a car crash that left Cleofas Guzman, an apostate union member, with permanent brain damage.

Chavez spent his last years protesting the use of pesticides in the fields. In April of 1993 he died.

The year after his death, Chavez was awarded the National Medal of Freedom by President Bill Clinton. In 2002 the U.S. Postal Service unveiled a thirty-seven-cent stamp bearing the image of Cesar Chavez. Politicians throughout the West and the Southwest attached Chavez's name to parks and schools and streets and civic buildings of every sort. And there began an effort of mixed success to declare March 31, his birthday, a legal holiday. During the presidential campaign of 2012, President Barack Obama designated the home and burial place of Cesar Chavez in Keene, California, a national monument within the National Park System.

The American hero was also a Mexican saint. In 1997 American painter Robert Lentz, a Franciscan brother, painted an icon, *César Chávez de California*. Chavez is depicted with a golden halo. He holds in his hand a scrolled broadsheet of the U.S. Constitution. He wears a pink sweatshirt bearing the UFW insignia.

That same year, executives at the advertising agency TBWA\Chiat\Day came up with a campaign for Apple computers that featured images of some famous dead—John Lennon, Albert Einstein, Frank Sinatra—alongside a grammar-crunching motto: *Think different*.

I remember sitting in bad traffic on the San Diego freeway one day and looking up to see a photograph of Cesar Chavez on a billboard. His eyes were downcast. He balanced a rake and a shovel on his right shoulder. In the upper-left-hand corner of the billboard was the corporate logo of a bitten apple.

# seven

# Disappointment

Though California has not inspired the finest American novelists, John Steinbeck's *The Grapes of Wrath* remains one of America's great novels. The native son imagined California from the outside, as a foreigner might; imagined wanting California desperately; imagined California as a remedy for the trial of the nation.

Otherwise, I might think of John Milton when I think of California and the writer's task. Milton devised that, after the Fall, the temperature in San Diego would remain at seventy-five degrees, but Adam and Eve's relationship to a perfect winter day would be changed to one of goose bumps.

The traditional task of the writer in California has been to write about what it means to be human in a place advertised as paradise. Not the Buckeye or the Empire, not the Can-Do or the Show-Me, California is the Post-Lapsarian state. Disappointment has long been the theme of California.

For example, my own:

I cannot afford to live here. I mean I do live here. I rent two large rooms. My light comes from the south. But if I had to move, I could not afford to live here anymore.

In San Francisco, small Victorians, small rooms, steep stairs, are selling for three or four million and are repainted to resemble

Bavarian cuckoo clocks—browns and creams and the mute greens tending to blue. That is my mood. If I owned one of the Victorians, I would, no doubt, choose another comparison. It is like living on a street of cuckoo clocks—and all the cuckoos are on cell phones—I won't say striking thirteen; nevertheless, a version of postmodernity I had not anticipated. Only well-to-do futurists and stuffed T-shirts can afford to live in this nineteenth-century neighborhood.

My complaint with my city is that I am old.

The sidewalks in my neighborhood are uncannily empty save for Mexican laborers and Mexican nannies and Mexican caregivers, and women wearing baseball hats who walk with the exaggerated vigor of a wounded pride (as do I). The streets are in disrepair; the city has no money; really, the streets have never been worse.

Can you imagine Adam and Eve grousing about run-down Eden?

California has been the occasion for disappointment since the 1850s, since men wrote home from the gold fields, from Auburn, from Tulare or Sonora, from tree stumps and tent hotels.

*I have no doubt I will prevail here, but you may not think my thicker skin is the proper reformation of an Ohio son. The men here are rough; they grunt and growl and guard their plates with their arms. Now I reach past my neighbor, and grunt, too, and shove, too, and I would cuss just for the pleasure of saying something out loud. I don't believe I have said more than ten words since I came to this place. I realize any oath I might devise would pale next to the colorful flannel they run up here. . . .*

And yet the streets are clogged with pickups and delivery vans, cable vans, and the vans of construction workers—certain evidence of prosperity. Crews of men, recently from old countries, work to reconstruct the houses of futurists—houses that were reconstructed not two years ago. One cannot drive down any street without having to go around the pickups and the vans, without muttering under one's breath at the temporary No Parking signs that paper every street, because everyone knows the only reason for the No Parking permits is to enable construction workers to drive to work.

Men from every corner of the world converged on the gold fields in the 1850s, prompting Karl Marx to proclaim the creation of a global society in California, a society unprecedented in the world up to that time. The gold parliament was an achievement of necessity as much as of greed.

Kevin Starr, the preeminent historian of California from the 1850s to the end of the twentieth century, has described California as a chronology of proper names: Stanford. Atherton. Giannini. Disney.

Disappointment came with arrival. Letters went out to the world, diaries, newspaper reports, warnings, laments, together with personal effects—eyeglasses, pen nibs, broken-backed bibles, Spanish Julia's beads—wrapped in soiled canvas. The stolen claim. Or the fortune squandered. (*Lottie, dear, I have wasted our dream . . .*) The trusting disposition. The false friend. The fog-shrouded wharf. The Spaniard Marquis, etcetera. The ring, the brooch, the opium den, etcetera.

Narratives of disappointment flowed eastward, like an auguring smoke, or bumped back over rutted trails, as coffins bump on buckboards, to meet the stories of the desolations of the prairie life, rolled over those, flowed back to the Atlantic shore, where the raw line separating the North and South was beginning to fester.

Nineteenth-century California rewarded only a few of its brotherhood, but it rewarded them as deliriously as an ancient king in an ancient myth would reward. The dream of a lucky chance encouraged a mass migration, toward *"el norte,"* or "gold mountain," or from across the plains of America.

For, as much as California's story was a story of proper names or of luck or election, California was also a story of mass— migrations, unmarked graves, missing persons, accidents. By the time he reaches the 1990s in his great work, Kevin Starr seems to sense an influential shift: The list of singular makers of California gives way to forces of unmaking—to gangs, earthquakes, riots, floods, ballot propositions, stalled traffic.

Disappointment is a fine literary theme—"universal"—as the young high school English teacher, himself disappointed, was fond to say, and it wears like leather.

Disappointment continued to be mined in California's literature throughout the twentieth century. Joan Didion gave us domestic broken-dreamers, not so much driven as driving. In the great Didion essays of the sixties, the mother abandons her daughter on the median of the San Bernardino freeway; dirty dishes pile up in the sink; the hot wind blows from the desert.

The Marxist historian Mike Davis gave us the California Club version of the broken dream—evidence on paper that a deal was cut. The water, the electricity, the coastline—everything can be bought or sold in the Promised Land, and has been.

California's most influential prose has turned out to be that of mystery writers, more in line with John Milton, who regard Eden as only an occasion for temptation and fall. For example, the eighteen-year-old cheerleader from Sioux City returns her en-

gagement ring, a poor-grade sapphire she got from a boy named
Herbert (not after the president); cashes in her scholarship to the
Teachers College; buys a ticket to L.A., enjoins herself to become
the new, the next—*Whaddaya think?*—Jean Harlow. (Ty Burr in
*Gods Like Us* remembers so many young women came to California, dreaming of stardom, that Hollywood denominated them as
"extra girls.") But the cheerleader ends up a manicurist in Van
Nuys; she ends up the blue, blond Jane Doe of the Month in the
Hollywood morgue. It requires a private investigator who is
broke, dyspeptic, alcoholic, but also something of a Puritan, to
want to incriminate California. The golden.

When she retired from the movies in 1933, Clara Bow told reporters: "It wasn't ever like I thought it was going to be. It was always a disappointment."

California's greatest disappointment essay is F. Scott Fitzgerald's *The Crack-Up*—an incautious memoir, meticulous, snide.

What an unenviable prospect, though, to be forced to listen to
the same lament—the Hollywood screenwriter's lament—at one
o'clock in the morning in the Polo Lounge. I once suffered a very
long evening thus, listening to a young man complain, in breath
that smelled of boiled eggs for lunch, about the difficulty of being
a "serious" writer in a town that idolized Spielberg. It was Spielberg that year; I imagine it still is Spielberg.

Francis Scott Fitzgerald at one o'clock in the morning:

*I saw that the novel, which at my maturity was the strongest and
supplest medium for conveying thought and emotion from one human being to another, was becoming subordinated to a mechanical
and communal art that, whether in the hands of Hollywood merchants or Russian idealists, was capable of reflecting only the tritest
thought, the most obvious emotion.*

Many decades after Fitzgerald cracked up, I saw with my own eyes a still orbiting fragment of his legend. I saw Sheilah Graham, a tarnished blonde in a black cocktail dress; she floated from table to table at Mr. Chow's restaurant, myopic, bending at the waist to kiss the air behind the ears of revelers. As a public sinner, she was something of a disappointment.

What Fitzgerald was too aureate to imagine was that unfastidious merchants of Hollywood—the ham-fisted, the thick-fingered, the steak-minded—nevertheless could pay somebody (scale) to develop the screenwriter's complaint into a script, into a picture about a pretty-boy screenwriter who ends up floating facedown in a swimming pool on Sunset Boulevard.

The question is: Does California have anything left to say to America, or to the world, or even to itself, beyond disappointment?

True, a vast literature is forming upon the Dewey-decimal Coast. Vietnamese-Californian, Japanese-Californian, Pakistani-Californian, Hispanics, all sorts, including my own. The question many people legitimately ask about this literature is whether our voices describe more than a hyphenated state.

My first literary recognition of California came from reading William Saroyan because Saroyan described the world I recognized. It was as simple as that. Armenian Fresno was related to my Sacramento. It was as simple as that—the extreme Valley heat (outlanders swore they never could stand it; or the flatness, either; or the alfalfa green); also the taste of water from a garden hose—the realization that California, that any life, that my life, therefore, was potentially the stuff of literature.

Here is the quote from Saroyan that I typed and pasted on the inside of my bedroom door, a manifesto:

*Try to learn to breathe deeply, really to taste food when you eat, and when you sleep, really to sleep. Try as much as possible to be wholly alive, with all your might, and when you laugh, laugh like hell, and when you get angry, get good and angry. Try to be alive. You will be dead soon enough.*

That was Saroyan's "advice to a young writer." I took the advice at a time when I had no expectation of being a writer or any desire or sense of obligation. It comes to me only now, as I type this, that Saroyan's advice has nothing to do with writing; it is advice for any mortal, sentient being.

It would be another two decades before I came upon the words that made me think I had a story to tell—the opening words of Maxine Hong Kingston's *The Woman Warrior:*

*"You must not tell anyone," my mother said, "what I am about to tell you."*

The immigrant mother's prohibition to her daughter reminded me of my own mother's warning about spreading "family secrets." In the face of California's fame for blatancy—in the face of pervasive light, ingenuousness, glass-and-aluminum housing, bikinis, billboards—Mrs. Hong recommended concealment. Her shrine is a published book.

About this time, Aram Saroyan, William Saroyan's son, published a bitter memoir of his father's last years.

William Saroyan was not on any syllabus I ever saw at Stanford or Berkeley, nor, incidentally, was Steinbeck. Stanford, Berkeley—these were schools established in the nineteenth century by professors from the Ivy League who had come west, like Peace

Corps volunteers, to evangelize California for the Atlantic Enlightenment. So perhaps it was not surprising that, even in the 1960s and '70s, very little attention was paid to California in any university course, despite the fact that California was in those years at the center of the national imagination. The only California novel assigned in any course I took, either in college or in graduate school, was Nathanael West's *The Day of the Locust*, probably because it fulfilled some East Coast expectation that California would come to doom.

And speaking of doom, the editor from *Time* magazine wanted an essay on California because it was a season (this was fifteen years ago) when the national newsweeklies were hitting the stands with titles like "Is the Golden State Tarnished?"

The *Time* editor wanted 750 words' worth of tarnish: "It would be nice if you could give us a Joan Didion essay."

"What do you mean?" I said.

"You know," she said. "Sardonic."

I unfold and refold that fraying *Time* story whenever I go to lunch with a California writer, handy to pull out if the conversation turns to New York. When the conversation inevitably turns to New York.

Anyway, California is getting too old to play the unhappy child or even the sardonic—too rich, too glued, too Angelica Huston walking substantially down some steps into the garden—to play the exuberant, the naïf. And California has grown children of her own. Two of the most interesting cities in North America are California daughters: Las Vegas, the open-throttled city, mimics California's youth, when land was cheap and cities were built in opposition to nature. Tijuana wants so little; she terrifies us for needing so much.

And: New York, truly, I am sorry to say, is not New York anymore. I say this having once been the boy who strained—the antenna on our roof raking through the starlight—to catch any shred of conversation from New York. I watched James Baldwin interviewed by David Susskind. I watched Norman Mailer chafing at America on *The Dick Cavett Show.* New York was a conversation. I guess I am stuck there. Buckley and Galbraith, Yale and Harvard, W. H. Auden and Hermione Gingold.

Unread copies of the *New Yorker* slip and slide on the opposite end of my couch—damn slippery things. Still, every once in a while an essential article. When I was in graduate school, and for many years after, the *New York Review of Books* fed my ravenous appetite for Oxbridge-Manhattan conversation. But then . . . what? I got too old; the conversation got too old. And surely the world must be larger than New York and London. Even now, I can pick up right where I left off: *SWM seeks SWF, for argument's sake.*

On an April day in 1970, I saw Dwight Macdonald. We both were stranded on a concrete island in the middle of Broadway. He was an old man in a raincoat in the rain. I was a graduate student. The rain was glorious, tall, immoderate. Everything was glorious. Broadway. No, I did not dare congratulate Macdonald for his bravery as a public intellectual, the best of his kind, and for whom the rain, that day, at least from the look of him, was just one more goddamned thing. Then the light changed.

Because Irving Kristol correctly predicted the light would change; that the intellectual center of America would shift from the shores of the Hudson to the Potomac.

For the writer, the problem of the absence of New York is the problem of the absence of a critical center, where opinion can be trusted to support talent or call down the falsely reasoned text. Washington think tanks are too far gone in the thrall to political power to provide that center. In the absence of critical structures, where does the young writer from California, or any writer, present herself for review; to what city does she apply for notice and contest? Nowadays, it is not Norman Mailer or James Baldwin who converse on television, it is Mitch McConnell or Harry Reid, and it is poor.

I was once interviewed on C-SPAN during the *Los Angeles Times* Book Festival. Five minutes max, the producer promised. Put this in your ear. Look over there. Five . . . four . . . three . . . two . . . I was standing on a crowded plaza at UCLA between two stalls, one for African American books, another for Latino books. I said to my interviewer, who was in Washington, DC, or a Virginia suburb, which was inside an electronic button, which was inside my ear, that I regretted these two neighboring book booths represented so little understanding of what California is becoming.

The earphone remained as neutral as a can opener.

. . . *I mean California's destiny is marriage. All the races of the world . . .*

Two-second delay. Obviously I have wasted . . . the earphone asked if I was going to attend the Great Debate.

*I'm sorry?*

"Our viewers are going to watch a debate between California and New York," the earphone enthused (a brightening of tone).

(California would be "represented" by Ms. Arianna Huffington; New York, by Mr. Pete Hamill.)

*You'd do better to stage a conversation between Duluth and El Paso.*

The earphone paused for an awful moment (*cf.* Bishop Proud-

ie's wife, *Barchester Towers* "suspecting sarcasm") before leaping
from my ear.

Americans have been promised—by God, by the Constitution of
the United States, by Edna Ferber—that we shall enjoy liberty to
pursue happiness. The pursuit constitutes what we have come to
call the American Dream.

Americans feel disappointment so keenly because our optimism is so large and is so often insisted upon by historians. And
so often justified by history. The stock market measures optimism. If you don't feel optimistic, there must be something wrong
with you. There are pills for disappointment.

The California Dream was a codicil to the American Dream,
an opening. Internal immigrants sought from California at least a
softer winter, a wider sky; at least a thousand miles' distance between themselves and whatever dissatisfaction they felt with
"home."

Midwestern California, the California of internal immigrants,
was everywhere apparent when I was growing up—in the nervous
impulse to build and to live in a house that had never been lived in
or died in; where the old lady never spilled milk, the dog never
died, the bully never lurked behind the elm tree; where widows
and discomfited children never stared at the moon through runny
glass, or listened to the wind at night. This California was created
by newcomers from Illinois and Nebraska, and it shaped my life.
This was California as America's America.

Simultaneous with Midwestern California was the California
of Maxine Hong Kingston and William Saroyan, and of my Mexican mother and father and my uncle from India; a California of
family secrets, yes, unorthodox ingredients—turmeric, cilantro,

curry, *Santa Maria Purisima*—but also some surpassing relief at having found in California a blind from tragedy. The relief California offered immigrants from other countries was comparable to the imagined restoration of the Joads. Though we lived next door to it, to the California of Nebraska and Illinois, ours was a California far removed from the drama of Midwestern disappointment, from the all-new-and-why-am-I-not-happy?

Thus, in my lifetime, I experienced two Californias concurrently. I discovered (because I was attuned to) a sort of hybrid of these two Californias in the writings of John Muir. Muir was born in Scotland; he moved with his family to Wisconsin when he was eleven. Muir saw California with a Midwesterner's delight in the refulgence of it—he called California "the grand side of the mountain." Yet I recognized in John Muir as well the quiet, grateful voice of the immigrant from overseas. Muir sailed into California. He first saw the coastline, as if through Pacific eyes; he saw immediately the implication of the coastline: California (and America) is finite.

When I grew up in the 1950s, freeways offered freedom from implication. California was neurotically rebuilding itself as an ever-rangier house in a further-flung subdivision. As a loyal son of California, I believed in all this, in the "new" and the other "E-Z" adjectives real estate agents employed to lure Midwesterners. And though the advertisement the real estate developer placed in the Midwestern newspaper was not a bluff, too many people believed, too many people came. The traffic on the freeway slowed from Jetsons to "Now what?" to Sig-alert.

What is obsolete now in California is the future. For a century and a half, Americans spoke of California as the future when they wanted to escape inevitability. Now the future attaches consequences and promises constriction. Technocrats in Sacramento warn of a future that is overwhelmed by students, pollution, immigrants, cars, fluorocarbons, old people. Or the future is diminished—water quality, soil quality, air quality, education quality, highway quality, life quality. There are not enough doctors for the state's emergency rooms; not enough blue parking spaces outside; not enough oil, not enough electricity. More blackouts, more brownouts; too many air conditioners, too few houses; frogs on the verge of extinction, a fugitive middle class. To the rest of the nation, California now represents what the nation fears to become. A state without a white center.

The brilliance of Midwestern California, the California that is founded upon discontent, and the reason why so much technological innovation springs from the West Coast, is that having confronted the finitude of the coastline, technologists in Silicon Valley have shrunk the needed commodity—the future (thousands of miles of Zen pathway)—to the size of a fleck of gold dust, to a microchip.

A few months ago, I went to have dinner in Menlo Park, where I met a young man who wore a linen jacket of the very blackest label and the scent of the winner's circle. He owns, very firmly owns, I imagine, on sheaves of legal-sized hard copy, electronic portals (virtual) through which the most ephemeral chatter and the finest thoughts of humankind pass as undifferentiated "content." I imagine Ensor's painting of *Christ's Entry into Brussels* at the Getty.

When I answered the young man's uninterested inquiry by identifying myself as a writer, his only response was to recommend I consign every published sentence I now guard with copyright onto the Web and give it away. *No one owns an idea in this age,* was his advice (and all of a sudden he sounded like someone one would have met on a riverboat). Except his idea, of course.

The young man's fortune comes not from the "content" his technology conveys, or conveys a quester toward, but rather from the means of conveyance—or, no, not even that. He will make more money by, at intervals, changing some aspect of conveyance or by padlocking the old portal (I imagine the Suez Canal) so that people have to pay to modify their means of access. He is set on weaning the minds of youth from the snares of merchandisers ("middlemen" he quaintly calls them). Young people are conveyed to the belief they should obtain intellectual property without paying for it, and without packaging. Packaging is sentimentality.

The young man is content to disassemble, by making "free," all intellectual property and factories of intellectual properties (recording studios, for example, or publishing houses), and all clearinghouses of intellectual properties (such as New York, such as Los Angeles, such as Harvard, such as the Library of Congress), in order that he can charge advertisers more for his arch or his gondola or his Victorian bathing machine.

The technologist now publishes to the world that place is over. California used to be the summation of the expansionist dream; now we foretell constriction. The future has been condensed to the head of a pin. Not Go West, not even Go Home. Rather, stay at home. Run in place. You are still connected, whether you are in the air or on a train or never leave Wisconsin. The great invention—rather, the refinement—of Silicon Valley is iPortability.

For a long season, California was the most important purveyor of narrative to the world. Hollywood was filled with stories in the last century, stories bought and sold, more stories than anyone could listen to or use. When other lures to California were exhausted or quieted down, Hollywood became its own narrative, became the golden dream; people wanted, literally, "to get into the pictures."

But in a California where place is irrelevant, narrative is finished. California is finished. (Narrative "takes place.") And whereas narrative used to take precedence, the argument in Hollywood now is not about the truth of a narrative, or even the salability of a narrative, but about which product format is going to pay off.

Toward the end of dinner, the optimistic young man from Silicon Valley, having imbibed a liter or so of Napa Valley pish-posh '69, got around to his detestation of the congestion of California. In the end, it would appear, he has to live in a real body, in real space, and in real time, and buckled into his hundred-thousand-dollar funk: "Traffic is a bitch every fucking morning."

. . . *When you get angry, get good and angry. Try to be alive. You will be dead soon enough.*

I, too, was an optimist. Well, I took Saroyan's pronouncement for optimism. Like many children of immigrant parents, Saroyan and I grew up among shadows, grotesque shadows thrown from a grandmother's stories, stories that might show us up as foreigners if they ever saw the light of day. How could the Saroyan boy in Fresno not be beguiled in the direction of games and sunlight? And then limelight? And then Paris?

I saw him once, in Tillman Place Bookshop in San Francisco, a bookstore made of wood, now long gone. He dressed like a stage bohemian; he wore a walrus mustache, and a fedora hat, and his cashmere coat rested upon his shoulders. He threw back his head to bellow, by which gesture he represented mirth. He was entirely admirable and theatrical. Saroyan's literary persona remained that of a carefree bon vivant, at ease with the world and delighted by it, tasting, breathing, laughing like hell. He'd never be a Princeton man—so what?

The legend: William Saroyan, the old man of Fresno, California, and Paris, France, was haunted by the early promise of himself. Critics had withheld from the middle-aged man the praise they once lavished on the youth. He was the same man. What gives? He became dark-minded and spiteful and stingy and mistrustful of friends and family and agents and stockbrokers and the IRS. The world smelled spoiled to him. He felt passed over by the world that mattered, the small, glittering, passing world.

The last time I was in Fresno, about a year ago, I gave a luncheon address at the African American Historical and Cultural Museum to a roomful of journalists from ethnic newspapers and radio and television stations. (The Pakistani radio station in San Diego. The Iranian television station in L.A. The *Oaxacan*. The *Mandarin*.) Everyone in the room spoke interestedly of a California that was crowded with voices, most of which they could not translate but they knew implicated them. No one knew what I was asking when I asked where Saroyan had lived.

The question for the night is the question of content, I think, not conveyance. A new generation of writers in California will not speak of separate neighborhoods, certainly not of brown hills and dairy cows, or of the taste of water from a hose, or of the sound of train whistles at night. Nor will they dote on New York, as I doted on New York. Oh, maybe they will, why deny them that? Perhaps New York will be Shanghai.

*In the time of your life, live,* was Saroyan's advice. I believe the difference between the literature of California's past and the literature to come will be the difference of expectation. There are children growing up in California today who take it as a given that the 101 North, the 405 South, and the 10 East are unavailable after two in the afternoon.

# eight

# Final Edition

A scholar I know, a woman who is ninety-six years old, grew up in a tar-paper shack on the American prairie, near the Canadian border. She learned to read from the pages of the *Chicago Tribune* in a one-room schoolhouse. Her teacher, who had no more than an eighth-grade education, had once been to Chicago—had been to the opera! Women in Chicago went to the opera with bare shoulders and wore long gloves, the teacher imparted to her pupils. Because the teacher had once been to Chicago, she subscribed to the Sunday edition of the *Chicago Tribune* that came on the train by Tuesday, Wednesday at the latest.

Several generations of children learned to read from that text. The schoolroom had a wind-up phonograph, its bell shaped like a morning glory, and one record, from which a distant female voice sang "Ah, Sweet Mystery of Life."

Is it better to have or to want? My friend says that her teacher knew one great thing: There was something out there. She told her class she did not expect to see even a fraction of what the world had to offer. But she hoped they might.

I became a reader of the *San Francisco Chronicle* when I was in high school and lived ninety miles inland, in Sacramento. On my way home from school, twenty-five cents bought me a connection with a gray maritime city at odds with the postwar California suburbs. Herb Caen, whose column I read immediately—second section, corner left—invited me into the provincial cosmopolitan-ism that characterized the city's outward regard: "Isn't it nice that people who prefer Los Angeles to San Francisco live there?"

Newspapers have become deadweight commodities linked to other media commodities in chains that are coupled or uncou-pled by accountants and lawyers and executive vice presidents and boards of directors in offices thousands of miles from where the man bit the dog and drew ink. The *San Francisco Chronicle* is owned by the Hearst Corporation, once the *Chronicle*'s archrival. The Hearst Corporation has its headquarters in New York City. According to Hearst, the *Chronicle* has been losing a million dol-lars a week. In San Francisco there have been buyouts and firings of truck drivers, printers, reporters, artists, editors, critics. With a certain élan, the *San Francisco Chronicle* has taken to publishing letters from readers who remark the diminishing pleasure or use-fulness of the *San Francisco Chronicle*.

When a newspaper dies in America, it is not simply that a com-mercial enterprise has failed; a sense of place has failed. If the *San Francisco Chronicle* is near death—and why else would the editors celebrate its 144th anniversary, and why else would the editors devote a week to feature articles on fog?—it is because San Fran-cisco's sense of itself as a city is perishing.

Most newspapers that are dying today were born in the nine-teenth century. The *Seattle Post-Intelligencer* died 2009, born 1863. The *Rocky Mountain News* died 2009, born 1859. The *Ann Arbor News* died 2009, born 1835. It was the pride and the function of the American newspaper in the nineteenth century to declare the forming congregation of buildings and services a city—a place busy enough or populated enough to have news. Frontier Ameri-can journalism preserved a vestige of the low-church impulse toward universal literacy whereby the new country imagined it could read and write itself into existence. We were the Gutenberg Nation.

Nineteenth-century newspapers draped bunting about their mastheads and brandished an inflated diction and a Gothic type to name themselves the *Herald,* the *Eagle,* the *Tribune,* the *Mercury,* the *Globe,* the *Sun.* With the passage of time, the name of the city was commonly attached to the name of the newspaper, not only to distinguish the *Alexandria Gazette* from the *New York Gazette,* but because the paper described the city and the city described the paper.

The *Daily Dramatic Chronicle,* precursor to the *San Francisco Chronicle,* was founded in 1865 by two teenaged brothers on a borrowed twenty-dollar gold piece. Charles and Michael de Young (a third brother, Gustavus, was initially a partner in the publishing venture) had come west from St. Louis with their widowed mother. In California, the brothers invented themselves as descendants of French aristocracy. They were adolescents of extraordinary gumption at a time when San Francisco was a city of gumption and of stranded young men.

Karl Marx wrote that Gold Rush California was "thickly populated by men of all races, from the Yankee to the Chinese, from the Negro to the Indian and Malay, from the Creole and Mestizo to the European." Oscar Wilde seconded Karl Marx: "It's an odd thing, but everyone who disappears is said to be in San Francisco." What must Gold Rush San Francisco have been like? Melville's Nantucket? Burning Man? An arms bazaar in Yemen? There were Russians, Chileans, Frenchmen, Welshmen, and Mexicans. There were Australian toughs, the worst of the lot by most accounts— "Sydney Ducks"—prowling the waterfront. There were Chinese opium dens beneath the streets and Chinese Opera Houses above

them. Historians relish the old young city's foggy wharves and al-
leyways, its frigates, fleas, mud, and hazard. Two words attached
to the lawless city the de Young brothers moved about in. One was
"vigilante," from the Spanish. The other was "hoodlum"—a word
coined in San Francisco to name the young men loitering about
corners, threatening especially to the Chinese—the most exotic
foreigners in a city of foreigners.

The de Young brothers named their newspaper the *Daily Dramatic Chronicle* because stranded young men seek entertainment.
The city very early developed a taste for limelight that was as urgent as its taste for red light. In 1865 there were competing opera
houses in the city; there were six or seven or twelve theaters. The
*Daily Dramatic Chronicle* was a theatrical sheet delivered free of
charge to the city's saloons and cafés and reading rooms. San
Francisco desperately appreciated minstrel shows and circuses
and melodeons and Shakespeare. Stages were set up in gambling
halls and saloons where Shakespearian actors, their velvets much
the worse for wear, pointed to a ghost rising at the back of the
house: *Peace, break thee off. Look where it comes again.*

I know an Italian who came to San Francisco to study medicine
in 2003. He swears he saw the ghost of a forty-niner, in early light,
when he woke in an old house out by the ocean. The forty-niner
was very young, my friend said, with a power of sadness about
him. He did not speak. He had red hair and wore a dark shirt.

We can imagine marooned opera singers, not of the second,
perhaps not even of the third, rank, enunciating elaborate prayers
and curses from the Italian repertoire as they stumbled among
the pebbles and stones of cold running creeks on their way to perform in Gold Rush towns along the American River. It was as
though the grandiose nineteenth-century musical form sought its
natural echo in the canyons of the Sierra Nevada. The miners

loved opera. (Puccini reversed the circuit and took David Belas-
co's melodrama of the Gold Rush back to Europe as *La Fanciulla
del West*.)

In 1860 San Francisco had a population of 57,000. By 1870 the
population had almost tripled to 149,000. Within three years of its
founding, by 1868, the *Daily Dramatic Chronicle* would evolve with
its hormonal city to become the *Daily Morning Chronicle*. The de
Young brothers were in their early twenties. Along with theatrical
and operatic listings, the *Chronicle* then published news of ships
sailing into and out of the bay and the dollar equivalents of treasure in their holds, and bank robberies, and saloon shootings, and
gold strikes, and drownings, an extraordinary number of sui-
cides, likewise fires, for San Francisco was a wooden city, as it still
is in many of its districts.

It is still possible, very occasionally, to visit the Gold Rush city
when one attends a crowded theater. Audiences here, more than
in any city I know, possess a wit in common and can react as
one—in pleasure, but also in derision. I often think our impulse
toward hoot and holler might be related to our founding sense of
isolation, to our being "an oasis of civilization in the California
desert," in the phrase of Addison DeWitt (in *All About Eve*) who,
though a Hollywood figment, is about as good a rendition as I can
summon of the sensibility ("New York critics") we have courted
here for 150 years. And deplored.

The nineteenth-century city felt itself surrounded by vacancy—
to the west, the gray court of the Pacific; to the east, the Livermore
Valley, the San Joaquin Valley, the Sierra Nevada range. Shipping
and mining were crucial to the wealth of the city, but they were
never the consolations the city sought. The city looked, rather, to
Addison DeWitt—to the eastern United States, to Europe—for ap-
probation. If there was a pathetic sense of insecurity in living at

the edge of the continent—San Francisco proclaiming itself "The Paris of the Pacific"!—the city also raised men of visionary self-interest who squinted into the distance and conceived of opening trade to Asia or cutting down redwood forests or laying track across a sea of yellow grass.

Readers in other parts of the country were fascinated by any scrap of detail about the Gold Rush city. Here is a fragment (July 9, 1866) from Bret Harte's dispatch to readers of the *Springfield Republican* (from a collection of such dispatches edited by Gary Scharnhorst). The description remains accurate:

> Midsummer! . . . To dwellers in Atlantic cities, what visions of heated pavements, of staring bricks, of grateful shade trees, of straw hats and white muslin, are conjured up in this word . . . In San Francisco it means equal proportions of fog and wind. On the evening of the Fourth of July it was a pleasant and in-structive sight to observe the population, in great-coats and thick shawls, warming themselves by bonfires, watching the sky-rockets lose themselves in the thick fog, and returning soberly home to their firesides and warm blankets.

From its inception, the *San Francisco Chronicle* borrowed a tone of merriment and swagger from the city it daily invented—on one occasion with fatal consequences: In 1879 the *Chronicle* ran an ex-posé of the Reverend Isaac Smith Kalloch, a recent arrival to the city ("driven forth from Boston like an Unclean Leper") who had put himself up as a candidate for mayor. The *Chronicle* recounted Kalloch's trial for adultery in Massachusetts ("his escapade with one of the Tremont Temple choristers"). Kalloch responded by denouncing the "bawdy house breeding" of the de Young boys, implying that Charles and Michael's mother kept a whorehouse in St. Louis. Charles rose immediately to his mother's defense; he shot Kalloch, who recovered and won City Hall. De Young never served jail time. A year later, in 1880, Kalloch's son shot and killed Charles de Young in the offices of the *Chronicle*.

"Hatred of de Young is the first and best test of a gentleman," Ambrose Bierce later remarked of Michael, the surviving brother. However just or unjust Bierce's estimation, the de Young brothers lived and died according to their notion of a newspaper's purpose—that it should entertain and incite the population.

In 1884 Michael was shot by Adolph Spreckels, the brother of a rival newspaper publisher and the son of the sugar magnate Claus Spreckels, after the *Chronicle* accused the Spreckels Sugar Company of labor practices in Hawaii amounting to slavery. De Young was not mortally wounded, and Spreckels was acquitted on a claim of reasonable cause.

When he died in 1925, Michael de Young bequeathed the ownership of the *Chronicle* to his four daughters with the stipulation that it could not be sold out of the family until the death of the last surviving daughter.

San Francisco gentility has roots as shallow and as belligerent as those of the Australian blue gum trees that were planted heedlessly throughout the city and now configure and scent our Sunday walks. In 1961 *Holiday* magazine came to town to devote an entire issue to San Francisco. The three living daughters of Michael de Young were photographed seated on an antique high-backed causeuse in the gallery of the old M. H. de Young Memorial Museum their father had donated to the city to house his collection of paintings and curiosities (including a scabrous old mummy beloved of generations of schoolchildren—now considered too gauche to be displayed). For the same issue, Alma de

Bretteville Spreckels, widow of Adolph, was photographed taking tea in her Pacific Heights mansion in what looks to be a fur-trimmed, floor-length velvet gown. The Spreckels family donated to the city a replica of the Palais de la Légion d'Honneur in Paris to house a collection of European paintings and rooms and furniture. One Spreckels and three de Youngs make four Margaret Dumonts—a San Francisco royal flush.

In 1972 the museum donated by Michael de Young merged with the museum created by the family of the man who tried to murder Michael de Young to become the Fine Arts Museums of San Francisco.

Men, usually men, who assumed the sole proprietorships of newspapers in the nineteenth century were the sort of men to be attracted by the way a newspaper could magnify an already fatted ego. Newspaper publishers were accustomed to lord over cities.

William Randolph Hearst was given the *San Francisco Examiner* by his father, a mining millionaire and U.S. senator, who may, or may not, have won it in a poker game in 1880. As it happened, young Hearst was born to run a newspaper. He turned the *Examiner* into the largest-circulation paper in San Francisco before he moved on to New York where, in 1895, he acquired the *New York Journal*. Hearst quickly engaged a yellow-journalism rivalry with Joseph Pulitzer's *New York World*. Both Hearst and Pulitzer assumed political careers. Hearst served in the Congress of the United States ("served" is not quite the word), as did Pulitzer, briefly.

We remember Joseph Pulitzer not as a sensationalist journalist but as the philanthropist who endowed an award for excellence in journalism and the arts. We remember William Randolph Hearst because his castle overlooking the Pacific—fifty miles of ocean frontage—is as forthright a temple to grandiosity as this nation can boast. And we remember Hearst as the original for Orson Welles's Citizen Kane. Welles portrayed John Foster Kane with the mix of populism and egomania audiences of the time easily recognized as Hearst. Kane, the champion of the common man, becomes Kane the autocrat. Kane builds an opera house for his paramour. Kane invents a war.

Citizen Kane told the story of a newspaper publisher's rise and fall in one generation. A more accurate rendition of the American newspaper saga would require an account of the long dissolution of the nineteenth-century enterprise. Although John Foster Kane has a son—we briefly see the boy, and we see that he will most likely be his mama's boy—the son is removed from the narrative early on (he dies in a car crash with his mother). We can only imagine that Kane's son, grown to manhood, might have resembled Otis Chandler, the utterly golden publisher of the Los Angeles Times, who, in retirement, was unable to prevent family members from selling the paper to the Tribune Company in 2000. The saga of American journalism in the twentieth century became a story of children and grandchildren and lawyers. McClatchy, Scripps Howard, Copley, Gannett—newspaper consortiums formed as families sold off the nineteenth century.

The San Francisco Chronicle and the San Francisco Examiner were both losing money when, in 1965, Charles Thieriot, grandson of Michael de Young, met with William Randolph Hearst Jr. to collaborate on what they called the San Francisco Newspaper Agency. The agency was a third entity designed to share production and administrative costs. The papers were to maintain editorial discretion and separate staffs. In addition, an incoherent Sunday edition shuffled together sections from both the Chronicle and the *Examiner*. The terms of the publishers' agreement eventually favored the afternoon Hearst newspaper, for the *Examiner* was soon to fall behind, to become the lesser newspaper in a two-paper town. The *Examiner*, nevertheless, continued to collect half the profits of both.

In January 1988, Phyllis Tucker, the last surviving daughter of Michael de Young, died in San Francisco. Tucker's daughter, Nan Tucker McEvoy, managed to forestall the sale of the paper for several years. But in 1999, the founding publisher's posthumous grip was pried loose by a majority vote of family members to sell. At that time, the Hearst Corporation was desirous of reclaiming the San Francisco market. Hearst paid $660 million to the de Young heirs for the *San Francisco Chronicle*.

To satisfy antitrust concerns of the Justice Department, the Hearst Corporation sold the still-extant San Francisco *Examiner* to the politically connected Fang family, owners of *AsianWeek*, the oldest and largest English-language Asian American newspaper. The Hearst Corporation paid the Fangs a subsidy of $66 million to run the *Examiner*. Florence Fang placed her son Ted Fang in the editor's chair. Within a year, Florence Fang fired her son; Ted Fang threatened to sue his mother. In 2004 the Fang family sold the *Examiner* to Philip Anschutz, a scattershot entrepreneur from Colorado who deflated William Randolph Hearst's "Monarch of the Dailies" to a freebie tabloid that gets delivered to houses up and down the street twice a week, willy-nilly, and litters the floors of San Francisco municipal buses.

The day after I was born in San Francisco, my tiny existential fact was noted in several of the papers that were barked through the downtown streets. In truth, the noun "newspaper" is something of a misnomer. More than purveyors only of news, American

newspapers were entrusted to be keepers of public record—
papers were daily or weekly cumulative almanacs of tabular information. A newspaper's morgue was scrutable evidence of the
existence of a city. Newspapers published obituaries and they
published birth announcements. They published wedding announcements and bankruptcy notices. They published weather
forecasts (even in San Francisco, where on most days the weather
is optimistic and unremarkable—fog clearing by noon). They
published the fire department's log and high school basketball
scores. In a port city like San Francisco, there were listings of the
arrivals and departures of ships. None of this constituted news
exactly; it was a record of a city's mundane progress. News was
old as soon as it was dry—"fishwrap," Herb Caen often called it.

Unwilling to forfeit any fraction of my quarter, I even studied
the classifieds—unrelieved columns laid out like city blocks:
*Room for rent. Marina. No pets. File Clerk position. Heavy phones.
Ticket agent for busy downtown box office. Must be bonded. Norman,
we're still here.* Only once did I find the titillation I was looking for,
a listing worthy of a barbershop magazine, an *Argosy*, or a Mickey
Spillane's: *Ex-Green Beret will do anything legal for cash.* Newspapers were sustained by classifieds, as well as by department-store
ads and automobile ads. I admired the urbanity of the drawings
of newspaper ads in those years, and I took from them a conception of the posture of downtown San Francisco. Despite glimpses
into the classified life of the city, despite the hauteur of ad-art
mannerism, the *Chronicle* offered some assurance (to an adolescent such as I was) it would have been difficult for me to describe.
I will call it now an implied continuity. There was continuity in
the comics and on the sports page, but nowhere more than in the
columns.

During Scott Newhall's tenure as executive editor, from 1952 to

1971, the *Chronicle* achieved something of a golden age. Newhall was flamboyant in ways that were congenial to the city. At a time when the *Los Angeles Times* was attracting admiration from the East Coast for its fleet of foreign bureaus, Newhall reverted to an eighteenth-century model of a newspaper as first-person observer.

For nearly two decades the city that prized its singularity was entertained by idiosyncratic voices. At the shallow end of the *Chronicle*'s roster (under the cipher of a coronet) appeared Count Marco, a Liberace of the typewriter who concerned himself with fashion and beauty and *l'amour*. At the deep end—a snug corner at Gino and Carlo's bar in North Beach—sat "Charles McCabe, Esq.," an erudite connoisseur of books, spirits, and failed marriages. Terrence O'Flaherty watched television. Stanton Delaplane, to my mind the best writer among them, wrote "Postcard"—a travel series with charm and humor. Art Hoppe concocted political satire. Harold Gilliam expounded on wind and tide and fog. Alfred Frankenstein was an art critic of international reputation. There was a book column by William Hogan and a society column by Frances Moffat. Allan Temko wrote architectural criticism against the grain of the city's sensibility, a sensibility he sometimes characterized as a liberal spirit at odds with a timorous aesthetic. All the *Chronicle* columnists and critics had constituents, but the name above the banner was Herb Caen.

Herb Caen began writing a column for the *Chronicle* before the Second World War. At that time, Caen was in his twenties and probably resembled the fresh, fast-talking smarty-pants he pitched his voice to portray in print. *Item . . . item . . . who's gotta item?* In 1950 he was lured over to the *Examiner* at a considerable hike in salary, and circulation followed at his heels. He knew all the places; he knew the maître d's, the bartenders, the bouncers, the flower-sellers, the cops, the madams, the shopkeepers—knew them in the sense that they all knew him and knew he could be dangerous. In 1958 Caen returned to the *Chronicle* and, again, circulation tilted.

Each day except Saturday, for forty years, Caen set the conversation for San Francisco. Who was in town. Who was in the hospital and would appreciate a card. Who was seen drinking champagne out of a rent boy's tennis shoe. His last column began: "And how was your Christmas?" He convinced hundreds of thousands of readers (crowded on buses, on the way to work) that his was the city we lived in. Monday through Friday, Caen was an omniscient table-hopping bitch. On Sunday, he dropped all that; he reverted to an ingenue—a sailor on leave, a sentimental flaneur infatuated with his dream "Baghdad by the Bay." The point of the Sunday perambulation was simple relish—fog clearing by noon; evidence that the mystical, witty, sourdough city had survived one more week.

After a time, Caen stopped writing Sunday panegyrics; he said it was not the same city anymore, and it wasn't. He wasn't. Caen was quoted in newspaper and magazine interviews admitting that Los Angeles, even San Jose—two cities created by suburbanization—had become more influential in the world than the "cool, grey city of love"—a George Sterling line Caen favored. The Chinese city did not figure in Caen's novel, except atmospherically—lanterns and dragons, chorus girls at the Forbidden City, Danny Kaye taking over the kitchen at Kan's, that sort of thing. The growing Filipino, Latin American city did not figure at all.

In Caen's heyday, the *San Francisco Chronicle* reflected the self-infatuated city. But it was not the city entire that drew the world's attention. In the 1950s, the version of San Francisco that interested the world was Jack Kerouac's parish—a few North Beach coffee-houses habituated by beatniks (a word Caen coined) and City Lights Bookstore. By the time I was a teenager, the path to City Lights was electrified by the marquees of topless clubs and bad wolves with flashlights beckoning passersby toward red velvet curtains. Anyway, the scene had moved by that time to the fog-shrouded Grateful Dead concerts in Golden Gate Park and to the Haight-Ashbury. A decade later, the most famous neighborhood in the city was the homosexual Castro District. San Francisco never seemed to grow old the way other cities grew old.

In 1967 the *Chronicle*'s rock and jazz critic, Ralph J. Gleason, teamed up with a renegade cherub named Jann Wenner to publish *Rolling Stone* magazine. What this disparate twosome intuited was that by chronicling the rising influence of rock music, they were effectively covering a revolution. In New York, writers were culti-vating, in the manner of Thackeray, a self-referential point of view and calling it the "New Journalism." In San Francisco, *Rolling Stone* was publishing a gospel "I" that found itself in a world without precedent: Greil Marcus, Cameron Crowe, Patti Smith, Timothy Ferris, Hunter S. Thompson. I remember sitting in an Indian tea shop in South London in 1970 (in the manner of the New Journal-ism) and being gripped by envy potent enough to be called home-sickness as I read John Burks's account of the Stones concert at Altamont. It was like reading a dispatch from the Gold Rush city.

One morning in the 1970s, the *Chronicle* began to publish Ar-mistead Maupin's *Tales of the City*—adding sex and drugs and lo-cal branding to the nineteenth-century gimmick of serial fiction. At a time when American families were trending to the suburbs, Maupin's novel insisted that San Francisco was still magnetic for single lives. In those same years, Cyra McFadden was writing sa-tirically about the sexual eccentricities of suburban Marin County in a series ("The Serial") for an alternative newspaper called the *Pacific Sun*.

In those same years, Joan Didion wrote in *The White Album* that for many people in Los Angeles "the Sixties ended abruptly on August 9, 1969, ended at the exact moment when word of the [Manson family] murders on Cielo Drive traveled like brushfire through the community." To borrow for a moment the oracular deadpan: In San Francisco, the sixties came to the end for many people in 1977, when Jann Wenner packed up and moved *Rolling Stone* to New York. As he departed, the moss-covered wunderkind griped to a young reporter standing by that San Francisco was a "provincial backwater."

What no one could have imagined in 1977, not even Jann Wenner, was that a suburban industrial region thirty miles to the south of the city contained an epic lode. Silicon Valley would, within twenty years, become the capital of Nowhere. What no one could have imagined in 1977 was that San Francisco would become a bedroom community for a suburban industrial region that lay thirty miles to the south.

*Don't kid a kidder.* Herb Caen died in 1997. With the loss of that daily hectoring voice, the *Chronicle* seemed to lose its narrative thread, as did the city. The *Chronicle* began to reprint Caen columns, to the bewilderment of anyone younger than thirty.

If you die in San Francisco, unless you are judged notable by our know-nothing newspaper (it is unlikely you will be judged notable unless your obituary has already appeared in the *Washington Post* or the *New York Times*), your death will be noted in a paid obituary submitted to the *Chronicle* by your mourners. More likely, there will be no public notice taken at all. As much as any vacancy in the *Chronicle* I can point to, the dearth of obituaries measures its decline.

In the nineteenth-century newspaper, the relationship between observer and observed was reciprocal: The newspaper described the city; the newspaper, in turn, was sustained by readers who were curious about the strangers that circumstance had placed proximate to them. So, I suppose, it is incomplete to notice that the *San Francisco Chronicle* has become remiss in its obituary department. Of four friends of mine who died recently in San Francisco, not one wanted a published obituary or any other public notice taken of his absence. This seems to me a serious abrogation of the responsibility of living in a city and as good an explanation as any of why newspapers are dying. All four of my friends requested cremation; three wanted their ashes consigned to the obscurity of Nature. Perhaps the cemetery is as doomed in America as the newspaper, and for the same reason: We do not imagine death as a city.

We no longer imagine the newspaper as a city or the city as a newspaper. Whatever I may say in the rant that follows, I do not believe the decline of newspapers has been the result solely of computer technology or the Internet. The forces working against newspapers are probably as varied and foregone as the Model T Ford and the birth-control pill. We like to say that the invention of the internal-combustion engine changed us, changed the way we live. In truth, we built the Model T Ford because we had changed; we wanted to remake the world to accommodate our restlessness. We might now say: Newspapers will be lost because technology will force us to acquire information in new ways. In that case, who will tell us what it means to live as citizens of Seattle or Denver or Ann Arbor?

The truth is we no longer want to live in Seattle or Denver or Ann Arbor. Our inclination has led us to invent a digital cosmopolitanism that begins and ends with "I." Careening down Geary Boulevard on the 38 bus, I can talk to my dear Auntie in Delhi or I can view snapshots of my cousin's wedding in Recife or I can listen to girl punk from Glasgow. The cost of my cyber-urban experience is disconnection from body, from presence, from city.

A few months ago, there was an item in the paper about a young woman so plugged into her personal sounds and her texting apparatus that she stepped off the curb and was mowed down by a honking bus.

When he was mayor of San Francisco, Gavin Newsom was quoted in the *Economist* concerning the likelihood that San Francisco would soon be a city without a newspaper: "People under thirty won't even notice."

The other day I came upon a coffeehouse on Noe Street that resembled, as I judged from its nineteenth-century exterior, the sort of café where the de Young brothers might have distributed their paper. The café was only a couple of blocks from the lively gay ambiance of upper Market Street, yet far removed from the clamorous San Francisco of the nineteenth century. Several men and women sat alone at separate tables. No one spoke. The café advertised free Wi-Fi; all but one of the customers had laptops open before them. (The exception was playing solitaire with a real deck of cards.) The only sounds were the hissing of an espresso machine and the clattering of a few saucers. A man in his forties, sitting by the door, stared at a screen upon which a cartoon animal, perhaps a dog, loped silently.

I should mention that the café, like every coffeehouse in the city, had stacks of the *Bay Guardian, S.F. Weekly,* the *Bay Area Reporter*—free and roughly equivalent to the *Daily Dramatic*

*Chronicle* of yore. I should mention that San Francisco has always been a city of stranded youth, and the city's free newspapers continue to announce entertainments for youth:

> *Gosta Berling, Kid Mud, Skeletal System El Rio. 8 p.m., $5. Davis Jones, Eric Andersen and Tyler Stafford, Melissa McClelland Hotel Utah. 8 p.m., $7. Ben Kweller, Jones Street Station, Princeton Slim's. 8:30 p.m., $19. Harvey Mandel and the Snake Crew Biscuits and Blues. 8 p.m., $16. Queers, Mansfields, Hot Toddies, Atom Age Bottom of the Hill. 8:30 p.m., $12.*

The colleague I am meeting for coffee tells me (occasioned by my puzzlement at the Wi-Fi séance) that more and more often he is finding sex on craigslist. As you know better than I do, one goes to craigslist to sell or to buy an old couch or a concert ticket or to look for a job. But also to arrange for sexual Lego with a body as free of narrative as possible. (*Im bored 26-Oakland-east.*)

Another friend, a journalist born in India, who has heard me connect newspapers with place once too often, does not dispute my argument but neither is he troubled by it: "If I think of what many of my friends and I read these days, it is still a newspaper, but it is clipped and forwarded in bits and pieces on e-mail—a story from the *New York Times,* a piece from *Salon,* a blog from the *Huffington Post,* something from the *Times of India,* from YouTube. It is like a giant newspaper being assembled at all hours, from every corner of the world, still with news but no roots in a place. Perhaps we do not need a sense of place anymore."

So what is lost? Only bricks and mortar. (The contemptuous reply.) Cities are bricks and mortar. Cities are bricks and mortar and bodies. In Chicago, women go to the opera with bare shoulders.

Something funny I have noticed—perhaps you have noticed it,

too. You know what futurists and online-ists and cut-out-the-middle-man-ists and Davos-ists and deconstructionists of every stripe want for themselves? They want exactly what they tell you you no longer need, you pathetic, overweight, disembodied Kindle reader. They want white linen tablecloths on trestle tables in the middle of vineyards on soft blowy afternoons. (*You* can click your bottle of wine online. Cheaper.) They want to go shopping on Saturday afternoons on the Avenue Victor Hugo; they want the pages of their *New York Times* all kind of greasy from croissant crumbs and butter at a café table in Aspen; they want to see their names in hard copy in the "New Establishment" issue of *Vanity Fair;* they want a nineteenth-century bookshop; they want to see the plays in London; they want to float down the Nile in a felucca; they want five-star bricks and mortar and Do Not Disturb signs and views of the park. And in order to reserve these things for themselves they will plug up your eyes and your ears and your mouth, and if they can figure out a way to pump episodes of *The Simpsons* through the darkening corridors of your brain as you expire (ADD TO SHOPPING CART), they will do it.

We will end up with one and a half cities in America. Washington, DC, and *American Idol.* We will all live in Washington, DC, where the conversation is a droning, never advancing debate between "conservatives" and "progressives." We will not read about newlyweds. We will not read about the death of salesmen. We will not read about prize Holsteins or new novels. We are a nation dismantling the structures of intellectual property and all critical apparatus. We are a nation of Amazon reader responses (*Moby-Dick* is "not a really good piece of fiction"—Feb. 14, 2009, by Donald J. Bingle, Saint Charles, IL, USA—two stars out of five). We are without obituaries, but the famous will achieve immortality by a Wikipedia entry.

National newspapers will try to impersonate local newspapers that are dying or dead. (The *New York Times* and the *Wall Street Journal* publish San Francisco editions.) We live in the America of *USA Today*, which appears, unsolicited, in a plastic chrysalis suspended from your doorknob at the Nebraska Holiday Inn or the Maine Marriott. We check the airport weather. We fly from one CNN Headline News monitor to another. We end up where we started.

An obituary does not propose a solution.

Techno-puritanism that wars with the body must also resist the weight of paper. I remember that weight. It was the weight of the world, carried by boys.

Late in grammar school and into high school, I delivered the *Sacramento Bee*, a newspaper that was, in those years, published in the afternoon, Monday through Saturday, and in the morning on Sundays. My route comprised one hundred forty subscribers—nearly every house in three square blocks.

The papers were barely dry when I got them, warm to the touch and clean—if you were caught short, you could deliver a baby on newspaper. The smell of newspapers was a slick petroleum smell of ink. I would fold each paper in triptych, then snap on a rubber band. On Thursdays, the *Bee* plumped with a cooking section and with supermarket ads. On Sundays there was added the weight of comics, of real estate and automobile sections, and supplements like "Parade" and the television guide.

I stuffed half my load of newspapers into the canvas bag I tied onto my bicycle's handlebars; the rest went into saddlebags on the back. I never learned to throw a baseball with confidence, but I knew how to aim a newspaper well enough. I could make my mark from the sidewalk—one hand on the handlebar—with deadeye nonchalance. The paper flew over my shoulder; it twirled over hedges and open sprinklers to land with a fine plop only inches from the door.

In the growling gray light (San Francisco still has foghorns), I collect the *San Francisco Chronicle* from the wet steps. I am so lonely I must subscribe to three papers—the *Wall Street Journal,* the *New York Times,* the *San Francisco Chronicle.* I remark their thinness as I climb the stairs. The three together equal what I remember.

# nine

# Transit Alexander

*a round*

*God formed you of dust from the soil. I was a sort of an afterthought. A wishbone. He blew into our nostrils the breath of life and there we were.*

*You were his Darling Boy and I was his Sweet Little Evie. The air was soft. We were made of clay. You were, anyway. He would hold up all manner of silly things he made for us, and we were supposed to name them with silly names. Everything we did seemed to delight him.*

*When he first showed signs of earthquake, at least I had the wit to say,* "Now which tree was that again, dear?" *But you just stood there with juice running down your chin.*

*God said to me:* I will multiply, multiply your pain from your pregnancy; with pain shall you bear children. *God said to you:* Damned be the soil on your account, with painstaking labor shall you eat from it, for from it you were taken. For you are dust and to dust shall you return.

*God made for us coats of skins and fur, and clothed us and sent us away.*

*Which is where we find ourselves: Nature runs through our bodies like rope. We give birth from our bellies. I do, anyway. We chew. We swallow. We regret. We decompose. These are laws of Nature. Natural laws are the brown laws. We hate them. We prevent birth. We eradicate polio. We clone goats and exchange hearts. We peer through our telescopes. We wear starched ruffs and underclothes. We compose divine comedies. Still, we must excuse ourselves fatuously whenever Nature calls.*

One day, Francis approached a bundle of rags on the road. The bundle of rags (there was a man within) commenced rattling a gourd. The gourd had pebbles inside. This served as a warning that the ragman was a leper. Lepers had bruised skins like the skins of pears. Francis left the road to the man of rags and walked another way for he feared leprosy above all things. But his fear of catching death that day was of exactly the same intensity as his attraction to the ragman's suffering. *Why should the ragman suffer?* Francis had walked into an equation.

He had to run to catch the leper up.

The bundle of rags recoiled from Francis's approach, whirled like a shredded felucca. Francis ran again and stopped once more in front of the leper. Francis took two thick coins from his pocket. He placed the coins in the road as if coins could tame a leper. Raising his eyes, Francis saw the ragman had no fingers, only two fibrous stumps, to one of which someone had tied the rattling gourd. Francis removed his kerchief and knotted the coins in it and tied the little purse to the leper's cloak. A puddle of urine formed at the leper's feet.

Francis took the leper's palm gently in his hand and raised it to his lips.

After the incident on the road, Francis embraced every leper he met. Francis began to call all creatures *brother* or *sister*. Francis began to dress in gunny in emulation of the poor. He slept under hedgerows and within the porches of churches; he had no more plan than a sparrow and the citizens of Assisi considered him foolish.

Uniforms often are brown, the common denominator. Workmen wear brown, many do. Department stores used to advertise "work pants" and "work shirts," usually khaki—a word from the Urdu, from the Persian, meaning "dust" and, in English, denoting a fabric of olive or yellowish brown. Sir Thomas More used the Latin word *cacus* to denote excrement, and English has kept the word as "cack."

The uniform of labor is a metaphor for singularity of purpose or function. The military uniform represents allegiance to an abstract entity, as if that entity were uniform. In a religious community, the habit, the robe, represents a vow to fit your body to an ideal. Your conception of fate, or love, or whether you like a skin of milk on your pudding is subsumed beneath your habit.

Navies wear blue. Land armies wear brown, as do the Franciscans. Uniforms, shaved heads, humiliations, acronyms are enlisted to turn singular lives into a manageable mass. Before the modern era, armies met at daybreak upon an open field. Because combatants needed to be able to distinguish an enemy, there were red coats on one side and blue coats on the other, as on the stage at La Scala.

Since World War I, land armies have clothed themselves in terrestrial disguise—uniforms are predappled with shade or prebleached into sand.

If you have seen the photographs of Spencer Tunick, whose one idea is to pose multitudes of nude bodies in parks and plazas around the world, you will have noticed that, en masse, in the uniform of nakedness, there is little discernible difference between tall-short, rich-poor, fat-thin, young-old, male-female.

We do not like other people to see what we are carrying. It is none of their business. We therefore carry boxes and suitcases, baskets, trash bags, trunks, purses, Manila envelopes, coffins. There is nothing more mundane than a brown bag lunch, nothing more intimate. The plain brown wrapper is a disguise and a discretion.

Brown can be a kind of fame, as well. As did the Franciscans, United Parcel Service has won brand identification with brown—with the color of cardboard and Kraft paper and clipboard. "Kraft brown" is a low grade of strong paper used for wrapping and bagging. Books used to be wrapped in brown paper, tied with string, and sent through the mail just like that. Commercial laundries used brown paper. I don't know how it is, but at some point laundry paper became blue. Whether brown or blue, such paper is ephemeral because it contains discoloring acids; it will deteriorate at a faster rate than paper from which acid has been removed. "Deterioration" is a brown noun of green virtue.

Carol Shields, in *The Stone Diaries*, wrote of "how fundamentally lonely it is to live inside a body year after year and carry it always in a forward direction, and how there is never any relief from the weight of it."

Brown attaches to pedestrian considerations. The soles of feet thicken from walking; they form a rind like citrus rind. Shoe leather thins from walking. Millions of people walk the earth on brown soles. It is a good feeling to have thick, dry soles. It is a miserable feeling to have cold, wet feet.

The sky is large and unimplicating. The road of life is one thing after another. Humans seem perpetually to be hauling property from here to there. There is a great movement of people across the continents of the earth—people who have been forced from their ancient beds by war or by famine or an empty purse, but also by curiosity. People steal over borders and wade through rivers and hide in bushes to show up at dawn on the streets of new cities, as if they have been there all along.

The soles of feet are maps of sorts, continents. We leave them behind eventually.

People in some cultures distinguish private life from public life by removing their shoes before they enter a dwelling. Ritual washing of the feet has significance for many religions of the world. We would wash brown away, whatever is sinful or sordid or earthly away, before we enter a place we hold sacred.

Moses must remove his sandals (for they are made of the dead) before he may draw near the Burning Bush, the presence of the Living God.

Do you imagine that some languages, dialects, inflections, are brown because of the complexions and not the pink tongues of the people who speak them? I have always thought American southern accents have less of landscape in them, or of color, than of humidity, drollery, time. Whereas a rich, rolling Burgundian accent sounds earthy to me. An Irish brogue—the dialect of spoken English of the Irish—is called, in English, by the name of an old brown shoe, "a rude kind of shoe" (*Oxford English Dictionary*), worn in the "wilder parts of Ireland" (*ibid.*). An Irish tongue is imagined to have clod clinging to it.

God commanded the Israelites to make a chest of acacia wood to proportions God provided. The chest was to have a skin of gold and on the lid of the chest two sphinxes of gold, their wings outstretched. Rings of gold were to be affixed to the sides of the chest, and, passing through the rings, two poles of acacia wood, one on each side, covered with gold. Thus would the chest be carried.

Into the chest the Israelites were to place the Tablets of the

Testimony of God given to Moses on Mount Sinai. Into the chest the Israelites were to place a vat containing flakes of manna, in order that future generations would see what Yahweh provided the Israelites in the desert.

The Word of God was thus a weight in the world to answer the question: Is God present with us or is He not?

The Word of God was a weight to be carried through the wilderness and to be housed in a tent of threads and colors and of a proportion God provided to the Israelites.

The Word of God remains a sacred weight for the descendants of the Israelites, as for Christians and Muslims. The five books of Moses, called the Scroll of the Law, called the Sefer Torah, dwell in a Tabernacle. Sefer Torahs are made by the hands of scribes who have studied patience, patience having the proportion and the duration of the letters of the living word.

This is how the Word of God is passed on: The scribe copies the words of the Torah onto a parchment made of the skin of an animal that one is permitted by the Torah to eat. The skin is split; the hairy side separated from the flesh-touching side. Parchment is made from the side of the skin on which hair grew. The skin is scraped with a knife. The skin must be cured using a mixture of gallnut and lime to make a parchment that is pliant and durable. Every segment of the parchment must be squared. Only black ink may be used, made of lampblack and gum and olive oil, and dried in a mold to a block; the ink is made fluid with water. The letters must be made with a stylus of wood or reed or the quill of a clean fowl. The scribe must pronounce each word before he writes it. Before the scribe may write the name of God, the scribe must say *I intend to write the Holy Name.* If the scribe makes a mistake of a word, the word may be excised by scraping it from the parchment with a sharp knife. If the scribe makes a mistake in making the

Holy Name, the segment cannot be used but cannot be consigned to fire or earth but must be placed in a storeroom for mistakes.

The segments are sewn into a scroll with threads of dry tendon of clean beasts. The scroll is affixed to two rollers of hard wood; the rollers are fitted with flat discs of wood on each end, and finials of wood or ivory. When the scroll is closed, the scroll is girded with a ribbon of silk and robed in a Mantel of the Law. When the scroll is closed, an ornament is fitted over the finials at the top. The ornament is called the Crown of the Law.

The Word of God is heavy, as heavy as a child of five years; as heavy as a man's severed leg, borne aloft. The scroll is unwieldy to carry, as unwieldy as a stack of forty plates. The scroll may not touch the ground.

If the honored man who lifts the Torah from the Tabernacle should make a mistake, if the Torah should sway, if the Torah should succumb to gravity, if the Torah should touch the ground, then not only the honored man must atone, but the congregation must fast from sunrise to sundown—their flesh will be subtracted from one day for having been careless with the weight of the Word of God.

Men and women consign the Torah to memory. The minds of men are as muddled as vats of glue. But the Word of God is justified, black and legible. Thus, not only by their backs do men bear the weight of the Word of God, but also in the scrolls of their memories.

In two clicks, I will find you an online Torah.

The majority of people who are alive do not find it impossible to believe that a computer can sort and sift, relay, recall, correct, cure, solve, destroy, filch, tabulate, and turn out the lights.

An increasing number of people who are alive believe that an all-knowing God—or let us say, an all-caring God—is an impossibility.

The computer is a diminishing physical weight and is not of flesh but is of synthetic or mineral substances. But the computer's content is enlarging, unstable, ethereal. I tap on the screen. I activate a sifting of digits—as many as the sands—digits align into commands that summon images of letters, black letters; black is itself a series of numbers—eventually a Torah. The computer cannot, though I can, pause to worship the Holy Name. One supposes a code might be written for hallowing the Holy Name—perhaps the letters could be made to appear to flame or to reflect a passing bar of light as do the simulated brass letters of the titles of TV movies.

Some American soldiers recently gathered several worn copies of the Holy Koran from the shelves of the makeshift library of a jail in Afghanistan. Someone had noticed the Korans had markings in them—words in the margins, highlighted passages. Perhaps the prisoners were passing coded information within copies of the Koran?

The soldiers took the sacred books and burned them in a bonfire.

I'm sure the soldiers considered burning to be an appropriate destruction of a sacred artifact. Americans consider flame to be a purifying element. What the soldiers did not stop to consider was that destroying the Word of God is an affront to God.

How can God be affronted by a couple of GIs building a bonfire? It is the faithful who are affronted on God's behalf.

The danger of weighted knowledge is literalism.

The danger of weightless knowledge is relativism.

The manufacture of my iPad, despite the fact that it is a miracle of weightless synthetic information, has already added burden to the misery of mankind. An item from the *New York Times* (I can easily find the date on my iPad; here it is—January 25, 2012): "Aluminum dust from polishing iPads caused the blast at Foxconn's plant in Chengdu. Lai Xiaodong was among those killed. He had moved to Chengdu, bringing with him his college diploma six months earlier."

Even now a pretty brown cow steps nymph-like through a green pasture in Shaanxi province; even now she takes the spirit of the living God into her delicate nostril. God knows she will soon be melted to glue, all unwilling, to bind this book.

*In the beginning was the Word: the Word was with God and the Word was God. . . . The Word was made flesh. . . .*

*Jesus said to Thomas: Put your finger here; look, here are my hands. Give me your hand; put it into my side.*

We will now rebuild the tree. The tree I have in mind will take thousands of trees and many years to build. I have a photograph before me of the Long Room of the library at Trinity College, Dublin, completed in 1732. The ceiling is a curved vault of candle-fumed wood. The floor is a plane of honey. The photograph shows a receding corridor on each side of which rise arched alcoves. Within the alcoves are shelves, from floor to ceiling. On the shelves are books bound in leathers of every hue, all brown. There are wooden banisters, benches, pilasters. The only appurtenances that are not brown are white marble busts of philosophers, poets, playwrights.

The room is massively silent. It ruminates upon a thousand forests and a thousand cities and personages, revolutions and plagues, ships lost and continents discovered. Sentences, formulae, drawings—knowledge is the sap of this tree. The tree is alive though all the philosophers represented by all the busts are dead.

The room will speak if questioned.

One of the earliest English definitions of brown—Samuel Johnson's definition—is of any color compounded with black. We have come to think of brown not only as a mitigation of black, but as an alternative to black, or as an abeyance. Love is stronger than death, say. Death being black. Or, beer does more than Milton can. Beer being brown. As if brown were a separate consideration. (*And malt does more than Milton can / To justify God's ways to man*— A. E. Housman's assertion.)

Earth is itself a canted color wheel, a cycle of vegetable, mineral, animal, and atmospheric accommodations to the Earth's passage around the Sun. The segment, the turn of the Earth, that corresponds to brown in the Northern Hemisphere is autumn. Consider, for example, the brown field in autumn, the stubble field. In climates where winter is cold, the autumnal field represents at once Nature depleted and Nature bountiful. There is something about the indeterminacy of brown that lends itself to such paradox.

She is the matronly season, Autumn, comfortable in her warm landscape. Ripe Autumn can nearly be heard to sigh: *Here will I rest a bit, my bounty is suddenly very heavy.* Her lids droop. Her smile is pleasantly hazy. Her days are shortening. But the sun is delicious. Isn't the sun delicious? Thoughts turn to elegy and apples. *Try one of these,* she says. Then, she says, *What do you suppose death is like?*

In September of 1819, the English poet John Keats, aged twenty-four, took a long walk before dinner. He was stopping for a time in Winchester. "I never liked stubble-fields so much as now," he wrote in a letter to his friend John Reynolds. "Aye better than the chilly green of spring. Somehow, a stubblefield looks warm—in the same way that some pictures look warm. This struck me so much in my Sunday's walk that I composed upon it."

Season of mists and mellow fruitfulness,
Close bosom-friend of the maturing sun

The ode "To Autumn" was written by a young man as if it were a young man's poem—Keats embracing his equation—as if the benediction of an ample day will not fail.

Still, not an autumn returns that I do not remember you by it, John Keats—that first day of which I am able to say: I can feel fall in the air. Though no longer young, I expect to rise in fall.

In 1625 John Donne, the English poet and Anglican priest, in a sermon at St. Paul's Cathedral, London, expounded on creation, as thus: When God made the world, he put into it *a reproofe, a rebuke, lest it should seem eternall, which is, a sensible decay and age in the whole frame of the world, and every piece thereof.*

In Los Angeles, on the hottest day of the year, the electrical grid surges upward in a digital tsunami, crests, browns out. The Kumtag Desert in China drowns the Silk Route, flows onward toward the city. Earth warms. Blankets of snow are thrown off. Rivers sink into their beds. Seas rise vertically like bamboo forests. Human activity forms an interesting brown cloak that floats over Lagos and Bangkok. Treacle-colored, coal-heated nineteenth-century London sounds wonderfully atmospheric in novels. But it was not wonderful. Eyes, throats, lungs burned; mouths blistered.

The first Earth Day was proclaimed, rather than astronomically calculated, by Senator Gaylord Nelson (D) of Wisconsin, at a conference on overpopulation in 1969. That same year, at a UNESCO conference, John McConnell, a California environmentalist, proposed a global Earth Day to coincide with the March equinox. Earth Day has evolved into an antihistorical celebration of prelapsarian Nature—Nature before human intrusion. The ideal human relationship to Nature, therefore, becomes one of corrective restoration. In the words printed on my cereal box: "Always leave the earth better than you found it." Green spring is an appropriate metaphor for the ambition of a perfectible world. Do not the branches of trees flounce about in pubescent green?

It becomes ideological to see brown as the harbinger of the end of Nature. But the bark of the tree—the wise part—forms protectively about the livid core. Surely autumn is as necessary a part of Nature as spring.

And brown has always been the sum of our breathing and eating and moving about. Even in the days of yore—days of *Odyssey*, days of *Gilgamesh*—smoke floated over villages and towns, heartening the traveler, still many miles distant.

There is a relationship, as young Keats noticed, between autumnal hues and warmth. One can certainly find a cold brown landscape. I grew up in such a landscape, one that might have been painted by Millet. When the fog rose from the fallow field, it was very cold in December. Even so, mine in the Central Valley of California remained, even in winter, a baked landscape. Nothing about it was raw. If only for its hue, it never appeared desolate to me. The earth was rich beneath its crust. I knew that if I dug down far enough—as far as gravediggers dig—I would find a room as warm as April.

I retain my liking for baked landscapes. For desert and the caramelized cities. Once, in an Italian hill town, on an uncomfortably warm August afternoon, I entered a restaurant, the only restaurant, where several clay ovens were blazing and citizens were ordering platters of roast pig for their Sunday dinners and drinking from earthenware jugs of cool wine. It was insanely warm. By and by, the room grew tolerable. I now declare I find the memory of it to be of exactly the right temperature.

There is evasion involved in cuisine, as with all human embarrassments, an evasion not of our cursed biblical state as grain-and-root-eaters (*from the soil shall you . . .* etcetera) but of our evolutionary, renegade taste for blood. Of ourselves as hunters. For we have not only the necessity to eat, the capacity to hunt, but also to pity our prey. Who does not pity the lamb?

Nor do I like to eat pale things. Poached eggs or fish or fowl. I want a buttered crust. I had an aunt who used to make a meal of boiled chicken with yellow skin and white gravy—and it nearly drove me mad to watch her. I prefer my warm-blooded fare to be certified cruelty-free, to arrive in unrecognizable "cuts" and yet to be served up with a purgatorial crust. I want malt *and* Milton.

In Kathryn Davis's novel *Hell,* there is a recipe for blancmange: Almonds are pounded to extract their milk, the milk is then strained, then sugar and transparent gelatin are added. The alloy is filtered once more through a white napkin.

> *. . . The resultant mixture . . . will be in fact utterly without texture, without substance, almost, you might say, without material existence, so that . . . to swallow it would be to swallow nothing, to attempt communion not with the body and blood of God's son but with the holy ghost itself . . .*

Chocolate, on the other burner, is one of the densest, brownest, most guilt-ridden substances we have learned to put into our mouths. It is also, curiously, one of the most refined—refined not from straining, but by compaction. Cacao was cultivated and eaten throughout Mesoamerica. In 1528 the Spanish explorer Hernán

Cortés transported the first cacao beans to Europe from Mexico. The refinement of chocolate proceeds as follows: The cacao tree puts forth pods. The seeds are harvested from the pods, fermented, dried, bagged. The chocolate manufacturer blends several strains of the beans for flavor and color. The beans are roasted and ground, then ground again to release their butter, then rolled around in drums and I don't know what all.

We relish taking in what most closely resembles—excuse me— what comes out. We are slow ovens. Ninety-eight point six. Brown is our biological point. Being alive depends on keeping warm. A warm room can be of any color, but heat feels brown, even though exhalations of breath on a cold morning are ghostly white. A bed as white as blancmange can feel as brown as a stable or a nest.

There exists a warm-blood club, no question. Warm blood might summon to your mind an albino bunny with red eyes, but the concept, you've got to admit, even if you have never taken a nap with your dog, even if your dog is black, is brown. And from warm blood comes sentimentality, which must be a vestige of fur.

No sober discussion of brown should omit mention of Marcel Duchamp's painting *Chocolate Grinder (No. 2)*, 1914, wherein three inexorable brown drums rest on a chassis that is elevated on decorative antique-moderne legs. The painting is beautiful; it is an accurate depiction of the physics of pressure. And it is ridiculous.

Now we will cut the wind from the tree. This entails killing the tree. Cut at the base. Birds fly upward. The tree may experience sorrow after its hundred amber-blooded years.

Cut the tree in sections, twelve feet long. Cut one of the sections lengthwise to appraise its grain—its diseases, indecisions, parsimonies.

Some years are deep brown cellos. Some, lithesome violins.

Some years are mantels or pillars or transoms. Some are ploughs and spoons for stirring. The rest is broom handles, toothpicks, clothespins. The rest is firewood and paper.

Take a block of the finest grain and carve of it a scroll. Make a thin slice of a softer grain, as thin as ham. And then another. And cut from these two scarab shapes for front and back. Cut it some gills. Bow its belly and thump its back. Seal, sand, varnish. String chords through the frets of its neck.

We will then recompense the wind and the leaves. We will make music.

In Manhattan, Billy Baldwin designed a brown study for Cole Porter—a famous room in the annals of décor. Ebony shelves were supported by brass piping. The dark walls were of tortoise-shell design on Chinese lacquered paper. There was a piano, several club chairs—this was a first-class cabin with no apparent clutter of creation.

The "brown study" is a term that originally referred to a state of mental absorption or abstraction. Etymologically, in this case, brown equals gloom. The fictional detective Sherlock Holmes was described by his fictional chronicler, Dr. Watson, as "in a brown study," a state of intense rumination, often accompanied by tobacco smoke, morphine, or Paganini. I wish now to conflate the term with the site. When Holmes and Watson first engaged rooms at 221b Baker Street, Watson described "a couple of comfortable bedrooms and a single large airy sitting room, cheerfully furnished, and illuminated by two broad windows."

Through many subsequent volumes of stories, the rooms darken considerably with the clutter of newspapers, chemical experiments, and notebooks—the clutter of overgrown boys—but also with an atmospheric residue of the contemplation of evil.

So that, in the ultimate volume, after many adventures, "it was pleasant to Dr. Watson to find himself once more in the untidy room . . . He looked round him at the scientific charts upon the wall, the acid-charred bench of chemicals, the violin-case leaning in the corner, the coal-scuttle which contained of old the pipes and tobacco." Holmes's study is a type of the necromancer's tower. Prospero's cell is another. The scriptorium of Saint Jerome. Merlin's cave. Faust's gothic chamber. Even Henry Higgins's library. The room represents the workings of the mind. The room must be untidy in order that mental abstraction will be orderly.

Sigmund Freud had two brown rooms. The first, in Vienna, where he invented a psychoanalytic method in much the same way that Conan Doyle invented detection—through an accumulation of case histories. The second in London. In either of Freud's brown studies, in both, books as well as prints and antiquities are displayed with an abacus-like precision. The seat of disorder in the room is a divan, covered with an irregularly patterned, plum-toned oriental carpet. Disorder enters Freud's study through a subject's subconscious.

There are substances that throw down roots in the human organism, roots that coil themselves around the little bones and dip their sharp nibs into the chemicals of the brain to draw up treaties, dependencies, visionary loans. Most of these substances are brown—brandies, whiskies, the sedimentary wines, opium, marijuana, coffee, tea. Among them the most delightful is tobacco.

Ass-eared leaves are harvested in sultry climes, cured to a golden brown, graded, then cut to various uses—pipe, cigar, cigarette, snuff. To ingest a lungful of tobacco smoke is to open an artificial bay, a small space of time, a monastery of privacy between one moment and the next, between one marriage and the next, between one sentence or one task and the next. It is unfortunate that tobacco is ultimately destructive of the organism it so be-friends. One's lungs become a shambles.

"You don't mind the smell of strong tobacco, I hope?" asks Holmes.

"Take the invalid to the sun," the gray doctor in nineteenth-century novels urges. The tubercular poet, against his better judgment, goes to Rome.

In the twentieth century, among light-skinned populations, a vogue for tanning began with the dawning age of tourism. The novelist goes to Mexico. Applying brown to oneself is different in its implication from painting health on one's cheek because it risks a confusion of racial and class identity. For the tourist, tan may be a mark of leisure. But tan is also the laborer's mark. In Cairo as in Quito, brown cloaks the distinction between the white-suited visitor and the company of criers and beggars in the bazaar.

In D. H. Lawrence's short story "Sun," a New Yorker named Juliet travels to Greece for a sun cure. Juliet takes the sun for a lover: "Sometimes he came ruddy, like a big, shy creature. And sometimes slow and crimson red, with a look of anger." Juliet's cure extends to a gardener she sees. She describes the gardener's attraction as "his vitality, the peculiar quick energy which gave a charm to his movements, stout and broad as he was." The reader is led to recognize the gardener as an amorous surrogate of the sun.

When the gods of Olympus sport with mortals, they take on the disguise of flesh:

Venus: *You see that girl?*
Cupid: (A vacant stare.)

**Venus:** *I overheard someone on the colonnade remark she has beauty to rival Venus.*

**Cupid:** *Surely not, Radiant Mother.*

**Venus:** *Oh, Radiant Mother! You know as well as I do the degenerates prefer that greasy sort of ripeness. Look how she goes. Inside, you know, they are nothing but filth. I want you to shoot her.*

**Cupid:** *She looks harmless.*

**Venus:** *She paints up, too. I've seen her at it with a turd of beetroot. They eat filth, they think filth, they make filth. They die in filth. Have you ever smelled one?*

**Cupid:** *Of course I have.*

**Venus:** *Do you like the smell of them?*

**Cupid:** *Not particularly. Apollo says you get used to it.*

**Venus:** *Apollo should keep his nose in the clouds where it belongs. I'll bet you've never smelled them when they cut their hair.*

**Cupid:** *Do they cut their hair?*

**Venus:** *Otherwise they look like complete monkeys. They have hair in the most comical places.*

**Cupid:** *Apollo says it tickles. If they are so beastly why do we wear their parts?*

**Venus:** *For sport. For butter. For fun. Form is nothing to us. Clouds. Trees. Thin air if we feel like it.*

**Cupid:** *Thin air is boring.*

**Venus:** *I want you to shoot an arrow through her big fat tit. The little idiot will fall head over heels for the first hairy back that flutters by.*

"Lend me thy cloak, Sir Thomas." The brown cape conceals the beggar-king, the sacred heart, the anointed head. Shakespeare's King Henry wraps himself in Thomas's plain cloak on the eve of the Battle of Agincourt in order that he might move unrecognized among his men. The twin device of disguise and epiphany is as old as the hills. Biblical Joseph is reunited with his jealous brothers. Richard the Lionheart reveals himself to Robin Hood. Caesar to Cleopatra. Arthur to Guinevere. Beast to Beauty. Cyrano to Roxanne. "It is I. All along, it was I."

Disguise is an attribute of the gods; modesty is not. The God of the Desert is an exception. The God of the Desert instructs that Aaron and his sons, and all priests following from their seed—"a law for the ages"—are to wear breeches of linen during sacred rites "to cover the flesh of nakedness; from the hips to the thighs they are to extend" in order that priests not flash their humanity during the gruesome work of the slaughter of beasts.

God's prescription seems only to confirm something that we already feel about ourselves, about our human nature, as represented by the flesh of nakedness from our hips to our thighs: that our private parts, as we call them, though definitively generic, are made of special stuff; are neither purely reflexive nor completely governable. We are confused. We are profoundly crafted.

The revelation of our nakedness to strangers, to lovers, has the potency of sacred awe, much like the prelude to a sacrifice. A hush falls upon the audience of a movie or a play when an actor disrobes. But when an actor appears suddenly naked, as if in the midst of life, the audience will laugh at its own embarrassment.

Even in a doctor's office, the moment of physical epiphany may be accompanied by a sense of awe. Young doctors of the twenty-first century resort to an Edwardian deportment at such times that one might call priestly. The patient feels herself a sacrifice.

In 1925, at the Théatre des Champs-Elysées in Paris, American dancer Josephine Baker appeared nude in a series of good-natured anthropological parodies. I quote Janet Flanner, the Paris correspondent for the *New Yorker,* who was there:

> *[Baker] made her entry entirely nude except for a pink flamingo feather between her limbs; she was carried upside down and doing the split on the shoulder of a black giant. Mid-stage he paused . . . swung her in a slow cartwheel to the stage floor, where she stood . . . an unforgettable female ebony statue. A scream of salutation spread through the theater. Whatever happened next was unimportant.*

Calvin Klein's notoriety came with his advertisements for male underwear in the 1980s. Klein employed the waxed, darkly tanned nude as both mannequin and garment. Underpants were a way of affixing a label to a body. Put on the garment and you put on nakedness. The notion that one's body could be worn (and not only one's body but one's tan, and not only one's tan but one's vacancy) became a conceit for a number of other designers, notably Gianni Versace. After Versace was murdered in Miami, frequent patrons of his Greco-carny boutiques received a memento mori in the mail—an album of flamboyant Versace designs interspersed with photographs of models wearing nothing at all.

Preindustrial populations wore furs and skins from practical necessity. Pelt was collateral to meat. We no longer need animal skins for warmth. In the city, therefore, a fur coat becomes a complicated conceit. Luxury merges with transgression. The socialite inhabiting the skin of a wild animal is enacting Beauty and Beast at once. If one were to play the conceit to the end, as Princess Diana famously did, one might visit one's reluctant paramour late at night wearing a fur coat, a diamond necklace, and nothing more. Queen and Huntress.

Long after Adam and Eve imagined they could hide from God, long before Princess Diana masqueraded as a predator, Queen Marie Antoinette dressed as an opéra comique shepherdess. The French speak of *nostalgie de la boue,* not with specific reference to *La Petite Ferme,* but applicable. Literally, *boue* is muck. What a splendid paradox, that a high civilization should cultivate nostalgia for a time opposite or before or below—a descent into uncivilization. Marie Antoinette as *boue*-peep, tripping through her Meissen barnyard, a little poetic fantasy within a political fantasy, within a world of filth.

We associate death with blackness because, I suppose, when we close our eyes we can't see. As to actual death, the death of a point of view—who can say? Death might well be as blue as a robin's egg. In the light of day the process of aging—and death itself—is brown. To the observer, death is brown. Time is bacterial progress.

In the cleaned, "original" version of the Sistine ceiling, Adam appears pale, beautiful, dead—his eyes do not yet see. The weather is fine. The void is a pale spring afternoon. Earth is green. The divine hubbub looks like the interior of a luxury sedan. God is massively potent and in love. Unborn Eve is tucked under God's arm, obviously a gift for the darling boy; she could be a nymphet on the cover of a Murdoch tabloid.

Sometime late in the 1980s, Pope John Paul II was consulted by a Cardinal Prefect concerning a proposal to clean and restore the frescoes of the Sistine Chapel. In the 1980s, John Paul was a vigorous, handsome man. In the 1980s, the ceiling of the Sistine Chapel had been left to darken for four hundred Roman summers. Michelangelo's Creation and Judgment wore the shadows of so many years.

At the apex of Michelangelo's grand design, God reaches toward

Adam to enliven him. In the damaged version, the four-centuries-old sinful version, Adam is brown, a figure of exhaustion; Adam seems to sink back into the earth upon which he reclines. God is prognostic, and his half shell of celestial hubbub shudders in turbulence. There are cracks in the void.

The Nippon Television Network of Tokyo proposed to pay for the restoration of the Sistine frescoes in exchange for exclusive rights to photograph the restored ceiling and walls. It took Michelangelo four years to paint the Judeo-Christian epic. It required more than double that time for the frescoes to be cleaned. Conservators used cotton swabs to apply distilled water to an acre of shale-like cloud. The Vatican installed an air-filtering system to circumvent any future deterioration of heaven.

In February of 1820, John Keats, aged twenty-five, suffered the first hemorrhage of his lung, losing eight ounces of blood. He left damp England on the urgent advice of his physician. By November he was living in Rome with Joseph Severn, a young painter who had accompanied him on his journey and who stayed on to care for him. Keats had a relapse in December and fell gravely ill. Keats forbade Severn to wish for a return of spring. Keats prayed each evening would be his last on earth and wept with each rising sun.

As a young man, Karol Wojtyła had been a playwright and actor of parochial repute. When Wojtyła became John Paul II, he became one of the great theatricals of his century. He played the Pope for the age of television. By the time he died in 2005, half the people alive on earth had known no other in the role. The planet his audience, the Pope seemed never without an intuition of the camera. Kissing the tarmacs of airports!

Those for whom decorum is a religion scorned the theatrical vulgarity of some of the trappings of John Paul II's papacy—the Pope-mobile, for example. But the planet loved it. The Pope-mobile served John Paul, as did the pop music, the lights, the windjammer chasubles, the stadium masses modeled after rock concerts.

During the final years of his papacy, John Paul II lost control of his person to Parkinson's disease; his speech, his movements, slurred.

Young Mr. Severn drew Keats in his bed—*28 January, 3 o'clock, morning: drawn to keep me awake; a deadly sweat was upon him all this night*. The sketch conveys the very smell of the night's ordeal. Keats's hair is damp on his forehead and cheek; his face is sunken; closed lashes darken the hollows beneath his eyes. The brown penumbra that circles John Keats's prone head seems to draw ink from his drowning breath. After the poet's death, Severn corrected his sketch to publish it as the formal pieta: *Keats on his deathbed, February 23, 1821.*

In her last decade, when the famous legs came unstrung, when the famous face could no longer be repaired, Marlene Dietrich hid herself from the eyes of the world. She became a prisoner of our memory of her face on the screen. She closed the drapes of her apartment on the Avenue Montaigne. John Paul II was the cannier theatrical. He was willing to portray suffering—dragged as he was through St. Peter's on a wagon, in a pointed hat, drooling. He found the spotlight. Here was Lear, here was Olivier; here was Samuel Beckett.

The Pope's last stage was his bedroom window, a perfect proscenium: The curtain opened. The old man was wheeled into the light of the open window to utter a benediction—his arm flailing uncontrollably, clutching his forehead in a simian gesture, his mouth opening and closing in tortured silence. The microphone was quickly withdrawn. The curtain began to close as the figure receded.

At the end of his life, in great bodily pain, Saint Francis had an intimation that he dwelled, on earth, already in paradise. Francis composed a summation, a prayer he called the Canticle of Brother Sun, wherein he commended and blessed his familiars: *Brother Sun, Sister Moon, Brother Wind, Sister Water, Brother Fire, and Mother Earth who nourishes and rules us*. As he lay dying, Francis welcomed one final aspect of Nature to his Canticle: *Be praised, my Lord, for our Sister, Bodily Death, whom no living man can escape*.

Toward the end of his short life, Hamlet, in a characteristically dark humor, traces for Horatio the ignoble decline of great Alexander. As thus:

> *Alexander died, Alexander was buried, Alexander returneth into dust; the dust is earth; of earth we make loam; and why of that loam, whereto he was converted, might they not stop a beer barrel?*

What clay should teach us to reply to Hamlet is that loam is as much the beginning as the end.

If you are afraid of its darker implications, it is not brown you fear but life.

# ten

# The Three Ecologies of the Holy Desert

*The curtain is down; its fringes are ripped; the curtain is patched and faded. From behind the curtain, there are sounds of a crowd, faint laughter. A dented brass band plays, ending with a drum roll. Mounting exclamations of concern and then tightrope silence. Amazements are in progress. A cymbal is struck followed by uproarious laughter and applause. The lights in the theater are extinguished as the curtain begins to rise. The only sound now is the buzzing of a fly. On stage, an old woman lies on a pallet on the floor of an empty room. A handkerchief covers her face.*

## 1. The Mountaintop

I wake up because the floor lamp in my bedroom has been turned on. (Passive construction indicates all that is seen and unseen.) It is three o'clock in the morning. My chest feels bruised, heavy. I am certain my mother has died.

Caveat: The lamp has a dimmer switch. My mother is in a hospital a few blocks away.

Several days later, I tell a neighbor, a man I know well, that my mother died and that the floor lamp in my bedroom came on during the night. My neighbor is sincerely sorry to hear of my mother's death; he supposes there must have been some kind of surge in the electrical grid.

Our lives are so similar, my friends' and mine. The difference between us briefly flares—like the lamp in my bedroom—only when I publish a religious opinion.

On June 17, 1992, Anita Mendoza Contreras was seated at a picnic table in Pinto Lake County Park, near Watsonville, California. Mrs. Mendoza Contreras was thinking her thoughts, as people used to say about someone staring out a window or worrying the hem of an apron, and among her thoughts were her children, about whom, for reasons of her own, she worried. She worried, and so she knelt down beneath an oak tree to pray. As she prayed, Mrs. Mendoza Contreras experienced a vision of the Virgin Mary. During the vision, Mrs. Mendoza Contreras's attention was fixed upon a portion of the trunk, high up in the spread of the oak tree. After the vision ended, Mrs. Mendoza Contreras saw that an image of the Virgin had formed within the bark of the oak.

Word of an apparition circulated somehow, and, the days being long, the nights being warm, people got into their cars after work and drove to Pinto Lake to see the oak tree with the Virgin's picture on it.

That is what we did, too—two friends and I—after an article about the image appeared in the *San Francisco Chronicle*.

The parking lot was a vacant field. I stepped in a cowpat. Federico Fellini, who as much as anyone entertained my adolescence and taught me the hope of magic, interjected into several of his movies comic scenes of crowd hysteria in the wake of miracles. As a worldly Roman, Fellini relished the humor of piety. As a Roman Catholic, as a lover of circuses, he shared the human need for marvels.

We saw people coming toward us who had already seen the

tree. They looked the way adults look—parents with young children—after an amusement has left them stranded: torpor, hunger, school tomorrow. Children were picking up acorns to put in their pockets. Already, I could see this wasn't going to be what I wasn't even aware I was hoping for.

Some women were sitting on aluminum foldout chairs, praying their rosaries in Spanish.

Easy to spot the relic tree within the grove because there were votive candles at its base. Boys with convinced expressions held compact mirrors with which they directed our eyes to the image by reflecting spangles of the setting sun onto the tree trunk.

I seem to remember there were already objects hanging from the branches—T-shirts, teddy bears, petitions—the forensics of hope.

I saw what they meant; I saw the shape. But I could not see what they saw. What Mrs. Mendoza Contreras saw. Though I, too, felt the need for visions that people brought to the tree and left there.

In the holy deserts of the Middle East, mountains rise from flat plains. It is on the mountaintop that God condescends and human hope ascends to within a hair's breadth of what humanity needs, what humanity fears. In the world's famous mountaintop theophany, Moses ascends Mount Sinai, under cover of cloud, to receive the Ten Commandments from God. The Israelites who wait below on the desert floor grow bored, unruly, forgetful of the wonders they have already witnessed. And that is the way of such stories. Heaven on one side of the veil; the field of folk on the other. Sometimes a souvenir passes from one side to the other.

We stayed half an hour; we stopped in Pescadero for green chile soup on our way home. No souvenir.

Another summer day: After the attack on the morning of September 11, someone posted on the Internet a photograph of one of the disintegrating towers. The image of a face seemed to form from whorls of black smoke—people were quick to say the devil's face. The face had a bulbous schnoz and more closely resembled the face of W. C. Fields.

Anyway, it was not Satan that people I know talked about in the days and months after September 11. It was religion—the religion of the terrorists—and the dangerous presumption of men who say "My God."

After September 11, it became easier, apparently it became necessary, for many of my friends to volunteer, without any equivocation of agnosticism, that they are atheists. It was not clear to me whether they had been atheists all along or if the violence of September 11 tipped Pascal's scales for them. People with whom, as my friend Will used to say, I would share my lifeboat, declared their loathing for religion, particularly the desert religions of the Middle East—the eagerness to cast the first stone, the appetite to govern civil society, the pointy hats, the crooks and crosses, the shawls, the hennaed beards. One of my closest friends, who lives in Memphis, observed that God looks to be deader than Elvis. (In his e-mail, my friend nevertheless resorted to a childhood piety: "God" is hallowed as "G-d.") But most of my friends left it at nothing. Whiteout. January First of the rest of their lives. (Buddhism retained its triple-gong rating.)

I was driving an elderly friend to a funeral. In response to nothing I had said (I suppose because we were on our way to a funeral), my friend announced her conviction that the world would be better off without religion. "I mean all of them," she said. An angry gesture of her open hand toward the windshield wiped them all away. As we drove on in silence, it occurred to me that I had interpreted what my friend said as something about men, though she had not said men. I had interpreted what she said as about God. But she said religion.

"I feel the same way about the Olympics," I said.

"Don't get me wrong," she said after a while. "I believe in the Good Lord. It's religion I don't like."

From his desert perch, a drab, plump ayatollah rejoices in the deaths of young martyrs who send infidel dogs to hell. The teachings of Jesus Christ go begging when a priest falls to his knees on the hard rectory floor to fondle and blight an altar boy's innocence.

My friend the doctor, whom I see every Sunday at Mass, whom I follow in the Communion line, asked, as we were leaving church, if I think the world is better or worse off for religion.

If you think the world is perfectible, then worse.


In American myth, the Village Atheist is a loner, a gaunt fellow in a flannel shirt, standing on a hill on Sunday morning. He faces away from the steeple in the dell. Perhaps he is putting flowers on his wife's grave. The hater of Sunday lives in a trim white house, eats porridge for breakfast; no wreath on his door at Christmas; gives generously to the Community Chest. His roses are the envy of the garden club, of which he is not a member.

Here are the three atheists of my youthful apprehension, apostles of the rounded sleep: Madalyn Murray O'Hair, Bertrand Russell, James Joyce.

Madalyn Murray O'Hair was a professional atheist who appeared on television talk shows in the 1950s and '60s. She was blowsy, unkempt; I could imagine her living room—the card table piled with legal briefs and Swanson TV Dinner trays full of pens and paperclips. She had two sons. Her fierce humor—I suppose I would now call it a lack of humor—was directed at Americans willing to violate individuality by insisting on public religious observance. O'Hair sued the Baltimore school system to outlaw the reading of Scripture in public schools; she sued NASA to stop astronauts from quoting Scripture in outer space. One of her sons repudiated her and she him; that son became a Baptist minister. Madalyn O'Hair was abducted by a former employee whose motive was, ostensibly, ransom. Her second son and her granddaughter were also abducted. All three were murdered.

In 1901, at the age of twenty-nine, Bertrand Russell discovered paradox. He wrote:

$$\text{Let } R = \{x \mid x \notin x\}, \text{ then } R \in R \Leftrightarrow R \notin R$$

Nor do I.

When I entered college, Bertrand Russell's book *Why I Am Not a Christian* stood face-out on the shelf of the campus bookstore—the face of a philosopher, I thought at the time. The face of an Anglican bishop, perhaps. The fluffy white hair, the starched collar. The face of an ancient satyr. In 1958 Bertrand Russell wrote: "I do not think the existence of the Christian God is any more probable than the existence of the gods of Olympus or Valhalla."

An affront to his ghost, I suppose, but Catholics, in our infuriating way, held out hope for James Joyce. Haunted, wasn't he? "Haunted" was the word we used. Old Jimbo exhausted his breath with sacrilege, yet the Church was forever cropping up in his book, wasn't it? He took it all too seriously, too young. Don't you worry, he'll have come round at the last, like Molly Bloom:

> *. . . as for them saying theres no God I wouldnt give a snap of my two fingers for all their learning why dont they go and create some-*

*thing I often asked him atheists or whatever they call themselves . . .*
*ah yes I know them well who was the first person in the universe*
*before there was anybody that made it all who ah that they dont*
*know neither do I so there you are . . .*

I have never been to the mountaintop, if that's what you mean. The only thing I know for a fact is that God never uses His own money. He hasn't got any money.

Some well-meaning person once referred to Dorothy Day, in her presence, as a saint.

"Don't call me a saint," Dorothy Day said. "I don't want to be dismissed that easily."

Dorothy Day, as one of the founders of the Catholic Worker movement, ran a hospitality house for the poor on the Lower East Side of New York. This was in 1956. The building that housed the hospitality house did not meet the fire code of the borough of Manhattan.

Dorothy Day was fined $250, which she did not have. The city ordered her to make repairs. The fine and the circumstance were reported in the *New York Times*. The same morning the *Times* article appeared, Dorothy Day was leaving the hospitality center for the courthouse in order to plead her case before a magistrate of the Upper Manhattan Court. A disheveled man in bedroom slippers stepped forward from a line of people waiting on the sidewalk for clothes to be distributed. The man handed Dorothy Day a check for $250.

The man in bedroom slippers was W. H. Auden, the greatest poet of his generation. Auden read the article in the *New York Times* while eating his breakfast, got up from the table, exited his apartment with a check in his hand, marmalade on his chin.

In a preface to a book of critical essays, W. H. Auden defined his vision of Eden (by way of divulging how his critical faculties were colored) as: "Roman Catholic in an easygoing Mediterranean sort of way. Lots of local saints . . . Religious Processions, Brass Bands, Opera . . ."

When I asked a priest-friend for his vision of paradise, he said: "Well, it will certainly be a surprise, won't it?'

*Wayne lived in one of the welfare hotels on Turk Street. He may have sold drugs; if he did, it was penny-ante stuff. He may not have taken drugs; he said not. Wayne was about seventy-five percent trustworthy, a rarified percentile. He couldn't read. I fear he may be dead. Wayne sat in front of the store across the way from Tillman Place Bookshop with a cup and a sign—he depended on fellow vagrants to make his signs for him:* VETERAN. GOD BLESS.

*Wayne was sweet-natured, simple-minded. Wayne told me he sometimes heard voices urging him to nefarious behaviors, but he refused those voices. He had no teeth, or few; he was often beaten up by bad men, particularly one bad man, who wanted Wayne's space in front of the store across the way. Wayne's space on the sidewalk was prime Sunnyside. The bad man, having chased Wayne away with hummingbird-like aggression, would then fold himself into abjection, would call out,* God bless you, sir, God bless you, ma'am, *to passersby, and he was, perhaps, an authentic agent of God's blessing, but not for Wayne.*

*On the day I recollect, the bad man was not about. Wayne was sitting on the sidewalk in his accustomed place. A droplet of rain was suspended from an awning; the tiny bag of water held the sun. A day in early January.*

*Switch-tense: As I watch, several things happen simultaneously: Up at the corner, in front of Shreve's, the old man who sings "When You're Smiling"—top hat, cane—is cajoling some frowning passersby to no avail. A young man—he is nobody I know—enters the scene from the north, approaches Wayne with a large pink box of doughnuts—left over from somebody's breakfast board meeting, I assume, then left out on a trash bin. Anyway, a box of doughnuts. The man seats himself on the sidewalk alongside Wayne, offers the doughnuts to Wayne and also a cup of coffee— so maybe I'm wrong about the provenance of the doughnuts. Wayne smiles with pleasure, catches my eye as he reaches for a doughnut, and is momentarily connected to the old man singing "When You're Smiling," for he and the other—the doughnut bringer—in mock-mockery, begin to sway to the cadence of the song like two bluebirds on a bough in a silly old cartoon. The sun, too, now seems a simple enough phenomenon—cadmium yellow pouring onto the pavement. A passerby drops a dollar bill into Wayne's cup and Wayne nods and smiles (and looks over to me). I smile. The design—tongue and groove—of a single moment.*

*I do believe the moment could be plotted algebraically according to some golden mean (though not by me), a line from A to B, B to C, C to D, D to E.*

*Therefore:*

$$A = B + C + D$$
$$B + C + D = E$$

*Therefore,*

$$A = E.$$

*But here's the thing: Wayne's smile.*

*I have thought about this for twenty years or more. Wayne's smile said: Do you get it? Wayne's smile said: Remember this moment, it contains everything.*

After September 11, atheism has become the most casual interjection into the television conversation. The grand old rock star OBE, for example, imparts to us, though he hasn't been asked, what he thinks of all that—of God, and all. *Well, that's all gone, thank God,* he says, slapping his shrunken thigh. The music critic in our local paper regrets, on his readers' behalf, the religious context weighing upon the transcendent beauty of a Bach cantata. And on the bestseller lists the ascending titles are apologies for the "New Atheism." From England, cradle of the New Atheism (as London turns Muslim and Hindu), Richard Dawkins, an Oxford biologist, proposes that parents who raise their children religiously are guilty of child abuse. On the same shelf, the journalist Christopher Hitchens titles his essay on atheism as a deliberate affront to Muslim piety. Roughly 145 years separate the bereft atheism that drummed upon Matthew Arnold's "Dover Beach" from *God Is Not Great.*

In the early 1970s, I was a graduate student at an institute in London founded by a German intellectual who went mad. He believed he was the god Saturn and that he had devoured his sons. The institute is devoted to the study of Renaissance intellectual history at the moment in Europe when magic became science.

The government inspector in Jean Giraudoux's play *The Enchanted* (1948) attempts to forbid the supernatural by decree:

> *Science . . . liberates the spirit of man from the infinite by means of material rewards. Thus, each time that man succeeds in casting off one of the spiritual husks of his being, Science provides him with an exact equivalent in the world of matter. When in the eighteenth century, man ceased to believe in the fire and smoke of hell, Science provided him with immediate compensation in the form of steam and gas . . . The moment man cast off his age-long belief in magic, Science bestowed upon him the blessings of the Electric Current . . . When he ceased any longer to heed the words of the seers and the*

*prophets, Science lovingly brought forth the Radio Commentator . . .*
*In place of revelation he now has . . . Journalism.*

On Bill Maher's cable television athenaeum, the journalist Christopher Hitchens proposes to Mr. Maher—and Mr. Maher wholeheartedly agrees—that science is the last best hope for humankind. Mr. Hitchens and Mr. Maher are unmindful, for the moment, of Hiroshima, drone missiles, chemical weapons, genetic modification, Original Sin.

After September 11, political division in America feels and sounds like religious division. Beginning with the sexual liberation movements of a generation earlier—with feminism and gay liberation—the growing preoccupation of the Left has been with the politics of sexual self-determination. There are some in the "old" political Left who decry the influence of sexual politics over traditional political concerns, like foreign policy and domestic poverty. It is more problematic that the new sexual identity movements allow themselves to be cast by the political Right as antireligious. The Left cedes religion to the Right, in exchange for a woman's right to legal abortion. The political Right intones Leviticus to homosexuals who wish to marry. The Right assumes a correlation between politics and religion; the Left assumes an antagonism toward traditional religion as the price of sexual freedom.

I am old enough to remember the Negro civil rights movement of the fifties and sixties. People who today relegate religion to the political Right forget how influential religion once was in the American Left. In those days, for that cause, civic protest was framed as religious idealism. Not only American history but salvation history seemed to weigh upon the present.

On television I saw Dr. Martin Luther King Jr. ascend the pulpit of the Mason Temple of the Church of God in Christ in Memphis. It was the evening of April 3, 1968. The civic life of America became part of a larger story, as Martin Luther King Jr. led his listeners to consider "the great and eternal issues of reality." He spoke of the exodus of the Israelites from Egypt; he spoke of Athenian democracy, the Emancipation Proclamation, FDR, and the Great Depression.

People said among themselves afterward that Dr. King's speech seemed, in its historical sweep, its elevated view, its summation, like the sermon of a man who knew he was going to die. Dr. King said he was grateful to God for allowing him to see this moment in America—the struggle for freedom by black Americans nearly completed. He said he might not reach the Promised Land with his people, as Moses did not. "But it really doesn't matter to me now, because I've been to the mountaintop," he said. "Mine eyes have seen."

### 2. *The Desert Floor*

The Israelites picked up a system of metaphor and a pervading sense of the irony of being God's Chosen from their sojourn on the desert floor—the desert floor as an unending test of endurance. For all the humiliations the desert inflicted upon them, however, it was from the desert that the Israelites projected, also, an imagination of the metaphysical world. Hell is hot, for example. Eden green. If the progress of our lives is a vale of tears, the Promised Land will be a psalm. All who are alive above the ground plead with the sky. But the Israelites alone among creation received an extraordinary assurance through the prophet Moses: Where does God reside? God resides with us.

A blessing upon the *New Yorker* magazine. The *New Yorker* con-

tinues to commission and to publish and to pay for original illus-
trations and comic drawings. I noticed, while thinking about this
book, that in almost any issue of the *New Yorker,* I could find cartoons that rely upon one of three allegorical ecologies that derive
from the religious imagination: Mountain. Desert. Cave. Three
ecologies of the holy desert still hold a place in the secular imagination of the Upper West Side.

The Mountain (these are drawings in the *New Yorker,* I remind
you): Moses raises his tablets. (Guy in the foreground remarks to
another guy, "Sans seraph!") The Hermit Sage is seated at the
mouth of a cave on a precipice—a foil to the Seeker who has
climbed the precipice to ask the meaning of life. The mountain
penetrates into the clouds to become Olympus, the mound from
which sausage-curled Zeus heaves thunderbolts. Cloud cover extends upward to the Pearly Gates and to Saint Peter's Desk, occasion for gags related to the bureaucracy of entry or exclusion, as at
a country club. Also, heavenly ennui—gags on the order of: *Not
what I expected.* Or: *If only I had known . . .*

The Desert: across which a Sun-Crazed Man crawls, or two
Sun-Crazed Men, one pulling ahead. Cactus, bones, empty can-
teens. *If only I had known . . .* Or: *If you had listened to me.* Also, the
Desert Island—a single palm, two strandees. *If you had listened to
me.* Also, the freeway exit to nowhere. (*If you had listened to me.*)
Also, the Crazed Miner, combining allegories of Desert and Cave.

The Cave: the Sage (*see* The Mountain). Or the Caveman—
usually a cave painter or an inventor of modernity. Also, the Tunnel of Love; also, the entrance to Dante's Inferno: *Not what I
expected.* Also, the Dungeon. Also, Hell—a vast cavern, lakes of
flame; themes of bureaucracy, ennui (*see* Saint Peter's Desk): *Not
what I expected. If only I had known . . .*

And I am forgetting one: Eden. *If only I had known . . .*

———

In his *Confessions*, Saint Augustine wrote of a "region of dissimilarity," an absence, a nonexistence, of synapse between his, Augustine's, ability to conceive and his attempt to conceive of the inconceivable—between the creature and the creator. "It transcended my mind," wrote Augustine of his intuition of God. "It was superior to me because it made me, and I was inferior because I was made by it." Augustine does not write about distance, but difference. We cannot think about God except insofar as God reveals God to us. And where did the God of the Jews, the Christians, the Muslims, reveal His intention to accompany us?

The desert is a region of dissimilarity to us, to what we need for life—water, shelter, a body temperature of 98.6. So, it is logical, in a way, to seek the unknowable in the uninhabitable.

The desert of my imagining is at once extraordinary—the locus of revelation—and ordinary; it is a plain, a disheartening expanse of time and the image of all our days. Such was the desert the Israelites wandered for forty years unchanging.

I found this in an old geography I was looking through the other day (*Man and the Earth,* Joseph Bixby Hoyt): "The desert has a strange fascination for many people, strange in that it is largely irrational . . . in the sense that the desert has little value for man, our interest may be considered irrational." The Bible and the Koran are deserts, irrational. The Bible thirsts for a promised land. The Koran thirsts for heaven. God yearns for his creation.

My brother is now seventy. His hands are burled with arthritis. Some days he walks with difficulty. Despite his present aspect, because of his present aspect and condition, I remember him as beautiful—my beautiful brother—which is the way our mother saw him, always. He was her favorite—and why wouldn't he be?— the firstborn, the son who made her laugh, even when she refused to smile.

When I was eleven or so, I went to the Monday-night wrestling matches every chance I got. A wrestler with woodpecker hair named Red Bastien used to climb to the top rope of the ring (as if despite audible huffing and puffing and manifest corpulence he had vanished into thin air) in order to leap down upon his opponent. I saw Red fly dozens of times. Until the year I saw Red Bastien, hair still red, leaning forward on a cane, as he hobbled across the lobby of the Memorial Auditorium. Red had retired from the mat to become a promoter. I was thirteen years old. I saw, as clearly as I would ever see, that the world passes. Red and I had been young together.

Jesus took three of his disciples—Peter, James, and beloved John—to the top of Mount Tabor. In the presence of the three disciples, Jesus was transfigured, passive construction; Jesus was revealed to his friends in something more wonderful than His earthly aspect. He shone. And standing to each side of Jesus was Moses and Elijah. They conversed! Peter suggested the disciples make three tents on the spot—one for Moses, one for Elijah, one for Jesus. Peter had no sooner conceived of an eternal moment than a cloud overshadowed the disciples. Within the cloud, the disciples heard a voice that frightened them, so they huddled together—all of a sudden, a warm-blood club against the supernatural. When the cloud dissipated, they saw only Jesus, the man whose smell and smile and hammered thumb they knew. Jesus told them not to be afraid. He said they must not speak of anything they had seen. They must all return to the valley floor.

In the Hebrew Bible, much of history is associated with life on the desert floor. Heroes become old men. Old men beget sons; sons lay their fathers down into the earth. Some sons find favor with God; some do not. On the plain in Canaan, the favored son, Joseph, is betrayed by his jealous brothers. He is sold to some passing traders, bound for Egypt.

I do not believe I was ever jealous of my brother. I acknowledged the justice of his preferment. My brother moved with such delightful ease. Where had he learned the secret of charming girls? Always girls.

My brother sits today at his computer and pounds, literally pounds, the elegantly argued e-mails (political argument) he posts to an electronic community in darkened rooms across America. (I imagine darkened rooms because correspondents are anonymous and because so many of these colloquia are nocturnal.)

My brother's politics are left wing, Democrat, in an easy-going way; lots of saints (FDR, Harry S. Truman, Adlai Stevenson). My brother's faith is that technocrats will lead us through a sea of red tape and partisan obstruction to the Shining City on the Hill. My brother's mind has long since turned against religion, particularly Christianity, particularly Roman Catholicism, and the Evangelical Protestants he calls "Christo-Republicans." My brother is an atheist, though that drab noun hasn't nearly enough pixels to portray my brother's scorn. He calls himself an "anti-theist"; he called himself that one Christmas evening, at the holiday table, as if he were the tipsy, freethinking uncle in a James Joyce short story; as if he were James Joyce himself.

In his senior year of high school, my brother announced he was going to enter the seminary in the fall. In those years it was not such an unusual thing for an idealistic Catholic boy—the class president, the football captain—to aspire to a life of heroic spirituality. *Ah, but he's giving up so much,* people would falsely lament— falsely, for they all knew there was nothing much in the great so-much. They meant he was leaving the mortal desert of sex and dirty dishes and the morning commute to climb, to begin to climb, the mountain. The inspirational climbers of that era were Thomas Merton (*The Seven Storey Mountain*), Dr. Tom Dooley (*The Night They Burned the Mountain*), and Dr. Martin Luther King Jr. (*I have been to the mountaintop.*)

My brother had been at the seminary for two years when, in his weekly letter, he informed our parents that he was coming home. A few weeks later I returned from school to find my brother's suitcases in the hall, his boxes of books. My brother must have given an explanation to our parents, but I never heard it. It was highly unusual for me not to ask, for I was the question man. But that is the curious thing about families, isn't it—how much one knows about parents and siblings, but also how much one will never know. Without losing any noticeable stride, my brother went on to college and law school and beautiful women.

During this period, my brother and I became rumors to each other. We could not have said, one of the other, on any given day, on which side of the country we were living, or with whom. We might see each other at Christmas, my brother affable, handsome, quixotic. My brother mentioned an important court case coming up. I told him I would pray for him. (Irony mixes fluidly with piety in our family.) No, don't, he said.

That's my brother the lawyer, at the wheel of his Porsche: His passenger is a stewardess from Lebanon. She is laughing; her languid arm drifts from the window as the Porsche pulls away.

A journalist friend assures me I don't know the first thing about deserts when I say I yearn to hike through the Rub' al Khali, the Empty Quarter of Saudi Arabia. My friend lived for several years in Saudi Arabia. The first thing about deserts, he says, is sand. Not sand as metaphor, but sand as irritant: Sand in your underwear, sand in your shoes, sand in the rim of the Coke can. He says to walk into the Empty Quarter is to journey into inchoate being. One feels dwarfed by emptiness, he says, as, he imagines, an astronaut must feel. "How could there be more than one God in such a place?" he says. My friend is an atheist.

This same friend also lived for a time in India. Such is India's comic fecundity, he says, that if one spits the seeds from a melon along the side of the road, then returns to the same spot the following year, one will find a constellation of golden fruit— dancing gods, he calls them—among the greenery springing from the ditch at the side of the road.

Several months ago, my brother sent me an e-mail concerning the Council of Trent, convened by Pope Paul III in 1545. If my life depended on it, I could not tell you what transpired at the Council of Trent. I noticed my brother sent copies of his e-mail to his nephews and nieces, as well as to our siblings. The wonder is not that he knows so much about Church history, but that such matters continue to preoccupy him. Why not let it go? The procession of our family continues, oblivious of the Council of Trent; there are baptisms, First Holy Communions, confirmations, weddings, funerals. My brother, the anti-theist, is always in attendance. That is he, photographed in a church pew, smiling. Next to him is his son. Me? Oh, I wasn't there. Out of town. Too distracted by my book on religion to show up for a grandniece's baptism.

I wrote to my brother a few years ago. I told him I was bored with his e-mails about religion. Bored with his scientific perspective, as he calls it. Bored with political faith. I asked him to stop.

Maybe the spirit of the times is to recoil from a mullah's absolute or a bishop's absolute, and to call that recoil atheism. Yet atheism seems to me as absolute as the surest faith.

As a Christian, I have so long sheltered in the idea of the God of the Jews, I would never think to call myself a theist. Too much abstraction is implied. I have buried both my parents "marked with the sign of faith." After September 11, I started describing myself as "Judeo-Christian-Muslim." Though I attend weekly Mass, I am struck by how often the priest, in his homily, must remind the congregation what we believe.

This year, the Catholic Church in the United States began using a new English translation of the Mass. The translation we had been using dated from 1973. The 2012 translation reverts to arcane English in an attempt to be more faithful to the Latin diction and syntax of the fourth-century Latin "vulgate" translation (from the Hebrew, from the Greek) of Saint Jerome. Why? I don't know. Why did Pope Benedict favor an eighteenth-century pattern for chasubles, as I have heard? And why did Vatican watchers raise their eyebrows at a Pope who favored an eighteenth-century pattern for chasubles? The Vatican must be more like a Ronald Firbank novel than we imagine.

Catholic journals blazed with controversy throughout that fall and winter. Many American priests, theologians, liturgists, and laymen objected to the new translation, particularly to the grammar of the Eucharistic prayer, which has taken an exclusionary meaning.

What I started out to tell you is that Sunday Mass has become a confusion, a bad lip sync. Some in the congregation continue to recite the 1973 translation—not out of refusal, but because humans are creatures of habit, and most of us have long since committed 1973 to memory. Some in the congregation resort to missals in the pews and follow the new translation scrupulously. Others, like the man who stands behind me, continue to pray in Latin.

The Creed (which comes early in the Mass) is the point at

which everyone stumbles. We used to recite the Apostle's Creed—rather, a version of the Creed closer to the Apostle's Creed, which dates from the first century. Now we most often recite the Nicene Creed, which was formulated in the fourth century as a refutation of the Arian heresy. The Arian heresy had to do with the divine nature of Jesus. The remembered lines are embellished with a few Latinate formulations that weren't there before, so we trip.

What is important to me is how important it is for me to be told what I believe. I could not, on my own, have come up with the two thousand years of argument that has formulated an evolving Christian theology. People who say of Catholics that we are told what to believe are correct. We are.

We are, most of us, not theologians. I borrow an excellent passage from an excellent pamphlet that was passed out to prepare American Catholics for the new translation. I cannot credit the author or the authors of the pamphlet, for there is no notation as to authorship or committee. The passage: "The Creed, or *symbolum,* is the symbol of our profession of faith; it is not the faith itself. We believe something because we first believed someone and that someone is Jesus." But before we get to Jesus (or Abraham or Moses or the Prophet Muhammad or Buddha) there is probably someone else. Mama. Papi. Miss Nowik. Nibs. Rabbi Heschel. Brother James. Jim Downey. Robert McAfee Brown. Flannery O'Connor. Father Costa. Andy Warhol.

My brother and I have, after many years, achieved our importance to each other as a difference. Because it is sometimes difficult for my brother to climb the steps to my apartment, he will often come by and we will sit in his car and talk. We quite enjoy one another's company. My brother is no less a good man for not believing in God; and I am no better a man because I believe. It is simply that religion gives me a sense—no, not a sense, a reason, no, not exactly a reason, an understanding—that everyone matters.

The congregation does not believe one thing; we believe a multitude of hazy, crazy things. Some among us are smart; some serene; some feeble, poor, practical, guilt-ridden; some are lazy; some arrogant, rich, pious, prurient, bitter, injured, sad. We gather in belief of one big thing: that we matter, somehow. We all matter. No one can matter unless all matter. We call that which gives matter God.

The moment of matter arrives with the Lord's Prayer. Jesus instructed, *"This is how you should pray: Our Father, who art in heaven . . ."*

The prayer takes about thirty seconds to recite, to join, in the present, the Christian world of centuries. It is the first prayer most of us committed to memory as children. It is the prayer most of us will say as we die. It is the prayer others will say over our bodies. The prayer makes no attempt to say what God is, but only what we are, what we need: We are hungry; we are sinners; we fear evil. It is the prayer that most easily takes us out of ourselves and joins us to centuries of people who have gone before, centuries of people who will come after.

That woman—five rows ahead on this side, red beret—her husband died of kidney cancer last year, yet here she is. The world ends. He is gone. She is here. I pray for him, her husband. What can that possibly mean, that I pray for him? I mean in a feeble, childish, desperate way (because there are people I believe I cannot bear to lose, and I imagine that woman feels the same, yet she has lost), I ask the hope of Enduring Love I call God to accept the man that was and to console his widow. Because the man who was is yet part of this day insofar as he is missing and she is here in her brave little red beret. Love is real. I have felt it, but I do not know how to live in love, once and for all, nor do I know if that is possible, though I have met people who almost seem to.

None of this happens as a forgetting of a day in summer, or winter, though there is that. I didn't leave the coffee pot on, did I? Shall I stop at the bakery on my way home? There is all of that.

The truest, most sublime vision of the Catholic Mass I have ever seen was in a Terence Davies movie called *The Long Day Closes*. The camera tracks over the heads of an audience in a movie theater, following the beam of blue light from the projector toward the screen, passing through the screen, then over the heads of the congregation in a Liverpool Catholic church, the congregation kneeling and rising as, all the while, on the sound track, the voice of Debbie Reynolds sings "Tammy."

This confraternity of strangers—the procession of the living with the dead—is the most important, most continuous confraternity in my life, though unpronounced except by rote prayer. I take my place in a pew as I would take a seat within a vast ark. Going where? We don't know. All we know is that one Sunday we will not be here. We know that nothing will change for our absence. Those are the names of the dead under the stained-glass windows and on all the tombs and plaques and rooms of testament and so forth, and so what? That is the consolation I take from the Mass—that I will join the obverse, which is represented to me by a lantern in a corridor that leads behind the altar. That I will join, for a while, the passive, prayed for. And then I will be forgotten. The procession will go on; it will emerge from the other side of the altar.

But not forgotten by God, please God.

And will there be an other, an active, present, everlasting love?

Eternity—which is a thought outside of time, isn't it?—need have no duration at all, I tell myself. Cannot, in logic. But that, too, is desperate.

And it doesn't matter a fig whether we say "worship" (1973) or "adore" (2012).

### 3. The Cave

In Israel, Jordan, Syria, Saudi Arabia, Egypt, one need only gaze up to see caves that were once chambers of an ancient sea—dry, riven sockets that seem to watch. The eye of the cave, however, is not the regnant metaphor. The mouth of a cave is what we more often say. The mouth of a cave is an image of perdition. We are organisms that sustain ourselves through our mouths. Indeed, we are caves ourselves. Since we eat, we fear being eaten. But we like the idea of secrets in the earth, of emeralds, rubies, sunless seas, for the womb is the cave we are born of.

Girls are taught early by their elders that their bodies are sacred caves, that they are, therefore, priestesses of some sticky magic and that boys are after stealing their magic. Boys are taught by their elders to mind the fact of their compulsion by Nature to enter that cave; that therein resides the meaning of manhood. Human innocence is calculated according to knowledge of the cave.

Mysteries and oracles abounded in the caves of the ancient world. Hindus and Buddhists revered caves as sacred sites, carved chapels in them and painted the walls. Because of the cave's long association with the esoteric and the supernatural, Plato took the cave as an allegory of unreason, of false apprehension. The prisoners of Plato's cave became unfit for any greater reality, content as they were to face away from the light of day and to consider only shadows.

Iegor Reznikoff, a musical anthropologist who has studied the resonance of cathedrals throughout Europe (by singing in them), has also explored the resonance of prehistoric caves. He has noticed that resonance in caves is often greatest or most pleasing in chambers with paintings on the walls, which suggests to Reznikoff a correlation between paintings and music. Caves were probably chosen for their resonance; probably they were used for chanted worship; probably they were painted commemoratively because they were places of ritual.

The book of Exodus, chapter 33, is nearly an inversion of Plato's allegory. Moses begged God to show him His glory. God refused—*No human can see Me and live.* But then God relented somewhat: *I will place you in a cleft of the rock, and screen you with my hand until I have passed by.* So it was that Moses withstood an experience of the ultimate reality by turning his back and shielding his face, much like the prisoners of Plato's cave.

A section cut away from the wall of a cave to reveal what is inside (like an X-ray view) became a prevalent conceit in early Greek-Christian iconography. Within the cave, the dead lie buried like bolts of cloth, or we see the hermit solitary at his prayer or we see the scull of Adam beneath the crucifix at Golgotha or we see the manger of Jesus.

The stable of Christ's birth was probably a cave that was used to pen sheep or goats or donkeys. The venerated site of the nativity in Bethlehem is the remnant of a rock cave. At the nether-end of the Christ narrative, six miles away, Jesus's broken body was laid on a shelf of rock in a cave, and it was there—in the darkness of that tomb—that light or voice or pulse or rush of wings found and raised him.

Since September 11, I have watched Muslims—Muslim men, I mean—at prayer with an admiration that is nearly unease. On Fridays, in the squares of the desert cities, men form themselves into rows, facing in one direction—a carpet of faith, a militia, if need be. It is not the posture of humility that makes me uneasy. It is the performance of single-mindedness that defines me as a spectator.

I pulled this instruction from the Internet. This is the proper way of performing Salah: *Stand at attention, put the world behind you. Then, creating tunnel vision, bring your hands to your ears, palms forward, thumbs behind earlobes* . . .

Prayer shawl, monk's hood, tunnel vision, the cloister of hands—the cave technique of prayer is common to all religions, all people.

The Prophet Muhammad hid from his enemies in a cave. In an hour's time, a spider sealed the mouth of the cave with a year's worth of web; the enemies of the Prophet passed the cave by.

It was in a dark cave that enlightenment came to the Prophet—that is the happy paradox of Islam. The gift of revelation was confusing and frightening to Muhammad; Muhammad described the imminence of revelation as like the approach of a concentric reverberation, as of a bell. *Read!* The Angel Gabriel commanded. The angel seized hold of the Prophet's body thoroughly, as though he would squeeze the Prophet's life from his mouth. *Read!* Muhammad pleaded with the angel; he could not read. *Read!* The Angel once more demanded. *Recite!*

The first revelation left Muhammad fearing for his sanity. He sought his wife, Khadijah; he trembled in her presence; he asked that she cover him with a blanket, as if that were a cave where the angel could not find him. It was Khadijah's faith that gave the Prophet courage not to deny or mistrust the revelation that had come to him. Henceforth, when Muhammad recited the revelations to followers, he would wrap himself in a blanket.

———

On a dark and drizzly morning in spring, I am delighted to find the garden snails schooning the sidewalk in front of my house. I suppose it is slickness that calls them forth. Lovely creatures like Viking ships. I pluck one up. *Surely you were better off where you were. What destiny summons you from the shelter of the underside of the leaf?* My impulse is to repatriate this pilgrim to the nasturtium patch in the park across the street—land of milk and honey (and probably slug bait). But I do not interfere. Despite the dangers, he is called. He has brought his cave with him. Even a snail must have a story.

As a very young woman, Agnes Gonxha Bojaxhiu journeyed from Skopje, Macedonia, to Ireland, because she had decided to join the Sisters of Loretto, a teaching order of nuns. She took the name of Sister Mary Teresa, after her patron saint, Saint Thérèse of Lisieux. Sister Teresa was sent by her order to St. Mary's Bengali Medium School for girls in Calcutta. She arrived there on January 6, 1929. Sister Teresa professed her final vows on May 24, 1937, after which time she was called, according to the custom of India, Mother Teresa. She was known among her sisters for her readiness to work and for her unfailing good cheer.

In September of 1946, on a train journey to Darjeeling for a week's retreat of prayer and reflection, Mother Teresa was inspired with the idea that she must leave the Loretto convent and venture into the slums of Calcutta to care for the poor of India. The inspiration was in response to a voice that spoke to Mother Teresa within her solitude. Teresa's rendition of the voice, in her notes and letters, has the urgency of a lover's groan. Mother Teresa characterized the urgency of the voice as thirst:

*My little one—come—come—carry me into the holes of the poor.—*
*Come be My light—I cannot go alone—they don't know Me—so*

*they don't want Me. You come—go amongst them, carry Me with*
*you into them.—How I long to enter their holes—their dark un-*
*happy homes . . . You will suffer—suffer very much—but remem-*
*ber I am with you.—Even if the whole world rejects you—remember*
*you are My own—and I am yours only. Fear not. It is I. . . .*

Mother Teresa confessed to her spiritual adviser, Father Van
Exem, that she had experienced a voice; she did not immediately
identify the voice as that of Jesus or, specifically, as it was in her
mind, the voice of Jesus thirsting on the cross. She confessed
she had conceived a desire to establish an order of nuns to serve
the poorest of the poor. She asked Father Van Exem to write to the
bishop.

There must always be a bishop.

Even divine inspiration, if such it was, must find its way around
a bishop. In Mother Teresa's case, the bishop was unmoved, un-
convinced, unwilling. Mother Teresa knew no better than to whee-
dle and plead in her letters. But it came to pass, as it must, that
divine inspiration—for such I believe it was—prevailed.

On August 8, 1948, Mother Teresa received permission from the
Vatican Office of the Sacred Congregation for Religious to leave
her order and to begin her new mission. On August 17, Mother Teresa walked through the gates of the Loretto convent, dressed in a
cheap white linen sari trimmed in blue, and with five rupees knotted in a bandana. The gates closed behind her. She was thirty-
eight years old; she was alone in vast India; she was a beggar.

If this were a film, I would pan backward at this point to show
the solitary figure standing outside the gates, on a street, in a
maze of streets, in the huge city smoldering in the mist of early
sunlight, to show how thoroughly this woman entrusted herself
to God.

The doors opened. Christopher Hitchens entered the elevator. He was smiling Felix-like; some thought or quarrel playing upon his lips. He smelled of liquor. And gossip. He carried some files under his arm; he had evidentially forgotten them, for as he lifted his arm to push a button on the elevator panel, all his papers fell to the floor. He bent over; I bent over to pick up his papers.

Mr. Hitchens was in New York for an international literary conference called "Faith and Reason," as was I. I suspect the organizers of the conference trusted their title to convey "Faith as Opposed to Reason," and they were not disappointed; the tenor of the discourse was irreligious. In another time it might have been assumed of such a gathering that writers would share, at least poetically, in the religious imaginations of their countries. During the three days I attended the conference, among the several hundred writers I met, only three confessed a religiosity that animated their fiction or non-. Indeed, so pervasive was atheism to the proceedings, a reporter from the *Frankfurter Allegemeine Zeitung*, who audited a panel discussion in which I took part, assumed I am and thus described me as a "non-believer."

Christopher Hitchens, a British subject who several years ago converted to America, earned his screaming-eagle badge by his support of America's war in Iraq—defending Churchillian saberlines in the sand. Before that endeavor, Hitchens became famous in America with an article he published in *Vanity Fair* attacking the holiest of cows, Mother Teresa of Calcutta. (A book on Mother Teresa followed: *The Missionary Position*.) Hitchens criticized Mother Teresa for accepting donations from persons whose fortunes were ill gotten; he criticized her for campaigning against abortion and birth control; he criticized her for gathering the poor to her death house, but not curing them; he mocked her for being an ugly woman. That last bit was, rhetorically, a reversion to the English public school sneer.

I suppose he was charming. Everyone said so. I didn't like him—I mean his public persona; I didn't like it. Still, his was a brilliant career at a time when writers do not matter much in the public life of America. Opinions on Orwell and Wilde with a Washington dateline are uncommon. As the Iraq invasion proved an exercise in neocolonial overreach, Hitchens, tripping over the stars and stripes in which he had wrapped himself, published a catechism for atheists called *God Is Not Great*. That book successfully reconciled Hitchens to bloggers of Left-lane bandwidth like my brother.

So, there we were, the two of us, stooping, improbably picking up a peck of (I presume) prickly papers as the elevator shunted us heavenward.

Hitchens straightened up; he smiled, mumbled thanks. The elevator doors opened.

A few years later Hitchens chronicled his cancer in *Vanity Fair*. He finished two books. He never backed down. He died on the front page. He reposes now in *Vanity Fair's* Tomb of the Well-Known.

Mother Teresa, the animus of so much of Hitchens's black ink, lived, by her own testimony, and for many years, in "terrible darkness," unable to discern the presence of God in her life. After Mother Teresa's death, a collection of her letters to various bishops, confessors, and superiors was published under the title *Mother Teresa: Come Be My Light.*

The most convincing aspect of Mother Teresa's story is the strangest: At the moment her request to establish a new order of nuns was granted by Rome and she was able, after years of petitions, to realize what she believed was God's will for her—the same moment we saw her outside the convent gates—God withdrew consolation from Mother Teresa's life. Henceforward, she must live in poverty of spirit; she must live, as so many live, without hope. She could not feel the once-proximate God; she could no longer hear the voice of Jesus. She did not doubt the existence of God. All she knew was that God had withdrawn from her personally. Several years later, in the tiny chapel of her fledging order, Mother Teresa watched the other nuns at their prayers. She wrote, "I see them love God . . . and . . . am 'just alone'—empty—excluded—just not wanted."

Darkness became the banal motif of Mother Teresa's life during her years of international celebrity, of flashing bulbs and television lights, of crowds applauding her entrance, of hands reaching to touch the hem of her sari. In November 1958, Mother Teresa wrote of herself in dejection to Archbishop Périer: "Our Lord thought it better for me to be in the tunnel—so He is gone again—leaving me alone."

So it was, also, with her namesake, the great small Saint Thérèse of Lisieux, who, in the agony of her death from tuberculosis, felt herself continually "in the night" or "in an underground passage." Gazing into the cloister garden, from her bed in the infirmary, Saint Thérèse noticed what she described as "a black hole" among the trees. "I am in a hole just like that, body and soul," she said. "Ah! What darkness!" In the final passages of her autobiography, Saint Thérèse likened herself to a small bird in a hedge that wishes to fly to the sun but cannot; she is too small, too weak. Dark clouds cover the sun. The little bird can no longer see the sun or feel its warmth; the wind blows cold; nevertheless, the little bird believes the sun is still there, behind the clouds. She will wait.

From Washington, Christopher Hitchens remarked that the

private letters of Mother Teresa proved her to have been a hypo-crite all along. "She was no more exempt from the realization that religion is a human fabrication than any other person, and that her attempted cure was more and more professions of faith could only have deepened the pit that she had dug for herself."

Atheism is wasted on the non-believer.

Until the end of her long life, Mother Teresa fed the poor; she gathered the sick and the dying; she cleaned and blessed the bod-ies of those whose deaths would not be mourned otherwise by anyone in the world.

Mother Teresa died on the night of September 5, 1997, in Cal-cutta. The electrical power failed in the convent in which she lay. The convent had two emergency generators, but they, too, failed. The breathing machine at her side was silent. She died in the dark.

*There is a rustling, as of silks; there is a tinkling of ornaments and bells and tambourines behind the scrim of heaven; a whispering, too, and a fluttering, as of birds in the rafters, foxes, mice, fairies, parakeets, rain; there is a sound of the flexion of tall trees, as the host of heaven assembles on risers behind the great curtain—a turning of halos this way and that, halos inclining toward one another in collegial candor, like interested sat-ellite dishes, and light shines from the parliament of faces as light from Pharos; lidless eyes these are, drawn with the black pencil of sorrow, the eyes of saints in icons, eyes that flamenco dancers also adopt to celebrate our passions as the victims of love on earth.*

# Acknowledgments

I am indebted to two editors at Viking Penguin, Kathryn Court and Ben George, for their editorial guidance, and for permitting me a literary freedom appropriate to an age when words literally mattered. John Jusino has been a special blessing—a copyeditor both sharp-eyed and sensitive, like no other I have ever worked with. Georges Borchardt, my excellent friend and literary agent, remains one of my best readers.

Besides being my intellectual conspirator and closest friend, Sandy Close, the managing editor of New America Media, financially supported the writing of this book.

Franz Schurmann and Alberto Huerta, S.J., were intellectual companions of mine for many years. Their influence on my thinking—evident throughout this book—survives their deaths.

I dedicate this book to my earliest teachers, young Irish women, members of the order of the Sisters of Mercy, who traversed an ocean and a continent to teach me. It was their lives and example remembered that has led me to the conclusion that the future of the Abrahamic religions will be determined by women, not men.

Jim Armistead, who, for more than thirty years, has completed my life, read and edited every page of this book with a rigor and compassion that define for me the meaning of love.